I'M NOT FINISHED

Sarah Merdian

JM Publishing
2011
Houston, Texas

JM Publishing
P.O. Box 4582 Kingwood Drive, Suite E306
Kingwood, TX 77345-2640
imnotfinished.smerd@gmail.com

713-896-9887 fax

13 Digit ISBN: 978-0-615-44900-5
Library of Congress #: 2011904706

www.SarahMerdian.com

Project Coordinator—Rita Mills
www.bookconnectiononline.com
Developmental Editor Peggy Sue Skipper
Cover Design—Warren Williams
WwPhoto3@cox.net
Text Design —Rita Mills

Back Cover Photo Courtesy of Uplift Education

The paper used in this publication meets the requirements of the American National Standard for Permanence of Paper for Printed Library Materials Z39.48-1984.
Printed in The United States

TABLE OF CONTENTS

Foreword   5

Introduction   7

Cast of Characters   17

Sarah's CarePage Journal   19

Afterword   215

    Charles Osterman   217

    Mary Merdian   220

    Emily Tamblyn   222

    Christine Garrett   224

    Karen Papania   228

    Laura Daly   231

    John and Deb Combs   234

    Tom Ballou   235

    Brent Hoelscher   238

From Sarah's CarePages Message Board   241

FOREWORD

I met Sarah when she was a freshman at the University of Dallas and I was the chaplain. From those early years I could see Sarah was different from so many of the students; somehow more confident, more outspoken, and possessing an amazing sense of wit and humor. I was blessed to have kept in touch with her over the years after graduation.

She eventually moved back to Dallas and we spent more time together. It was then that she was first diagnosed. I remember her laughing and telling me how she figured that now she could have an edge on getting what she wanted, "I have cancer and I want..!

As the months and the disease progressed she asked to "talk", an unusual request from someone so self assured. What she expressed was that she was worried and in pain, but it was not the pain that others in her situation usually speak about. She explained that so many people were telling her that they were praying for her and that God would heal her. They were saying that they knew she would beat this. But she explained what if that is not the way it works out, what if I do die, how will my friends deal with their pain. She then asked what she could do to help her friends through this. The stage was set for the amazing story of Sarah's illness and how through her writing during that time awakened in us the healing power of friendship, acceptance, and love.

Msgr. Donald L. Fischer, *President*
Pastoral Reflections Institute
Dallas, Texas

Sarah's words whether in the form of poetry or journal entries give rare insight into the life of a cancer survivor. Sarah had the ability to capture the ups and downs of a person wrestling with the cascading side effects of chemotherapy or the myriad of emotional and spiritual responses to recurrence. I was so impressed by Sarah's ability to reflect on her own experience, no matter how chaotic, that I use Sarah's poetry to educate and awaken caregivers to the human embodiment of the cancer experience.

Chaplain Alan Wright, *M.Div, BCC*
Charles A. Sammons Cancer Center
Baylor University Medical Center

INTRODUCTION

> *All journeys have secret destinations of which the traveler is unaware.* —Martin Buber

2010 estimates of new cancer cases to be diagnosed[1]:

- 1,529,560 all types 39% will die.
- 21,880 ovarian 63% will die.
- 43,470 uterine 18.6% will die

On August 7, 2008, my older daughter, Sarah, became one of the gruesome "will die" statistics for both uterine[2] and ovarian cancers.

If you or someone in your circle of life is a member of that statistical class, you really should read this book. Traveling with Sarah Merdian during her final 18 months will take you geographically to Beijing, The Great Wall, Prague, Czech Republic, Hawaii, New York City, Denver and Texas. Emotionally, you will visit a state of grace under fire, the depths of courage, the heights of laughter and a razor sharp wit.

Sarah used the CarePages[3] website (CarePages.com—SarahMerdian) to maintain that life-giving contact with her family and many friends around the world. Her CarePage had 1468 visits!!! Kudos to Mary and Mim for making CarePages possible and a special thanks to Mary for being the Scribner when Sarah couldn't.

CarePages is an electronic marvel! Each posting provided the benefit of Sarah's wit and wisdom, her ability to find joy in the mundane, and her indomitable will to stay true to herself. You can also view and experience the messages posted by Sarah's friends, as well as individuals who only knew Sarah through her CarePage postings

Publishing Sarah's CarePage postings as *I'm Not Finished* was her idea in response to many encouraging words from family, friends, and caregivers. She just didn't have enough time or energy to complete the project. In true Sarah style, she gave me explicit instructions (size, type, title, format) and charged me with completing the task. Overall, her instructions were "Keep It Simple" just like the title to Van Morrison's 2008 CD. Van Morrison was one of Sarah's favorite artists and his music provided much support during her last months. The Baylor—Dallas chaplain uses Sarah's commentary on chemo and its after-effects in his cancer support sessions. A friend's mother told me Sarah's words provided the courage to face her fourth round of chemo.

I have received much encouragement and support from near and far in keeping my promise to Sarah to publish "INF". Without naming names (the list is just too long and you know who you are), I am grateful for your patience, your encouraging words and your tangible support.

I won't pretend to be totally objective. After all, Sarah was my older daughter and motherhood permits a certain degree of subjectivity. This is I do know for fact:

- At 9 months Sarah just stood up from a crawling position and walked. The first step of a whirlwind, worldwide journey across many continents.

- At age 13, Sarah and her friend, Wendy, decided they were "too old to play all summer." They planned and executed a window washing endeavor to occupy themselves and make a little spending money. They just needed the mothers for transportation as they already had jobs scheduled with local realtors. The first of many "never sit around or stay at home" summers.

• Tenth grade Sarah had her plan. College in Texas and then law school in Texas. She even had her budget for first year college committed to paper.

• During high school, Sarah was on "honors track". Classes were 7 am to noon. Three to four days a week, she went straight to Long John Silver's and worked the afternoon shift (never liked cole slaw afterwards). At 16, she had money saved to buy her first car (VW Bug), pay for insurance and escrow for repairs.

• 1978 Sarah graduated with honors from Putnam City High School, Oklahoma City and (perhaps because of her numerous extra-curricular activities Sunday School teacher, summer camp counselor, church youth music group (guitar), pep squad, French Club, National Honor Society), was awarded a full scholarship at the University of Dallas. After she accepted the scholarship, we found out about UD's "Rome program" which would fulfill a dream of hers since middle school to travel to France and Italy.

• In August 1979, Sarah and about 100 fellow UD sophomores went to Rome for a semester. An amazing friendship bond had its nucleus in that experience. In this book, you will encounter Charles, Dan (and his five siblings all—UDers), Karen and Deb (roommates),

Deb's husband John, and Laura, along with many others who are connected to UD either by alumna status or by marriage. I don't have adequate words to describe the loving, caring, irreverent, hilarious relationships. The "friends" convene twice yearly (December and Summer) from all over the globe. They also respond to one another according to some secret code of caring and support. An Amazing Community which Sarah and I affectionately referred to as the "UD Bunch". I have been the collateral beneficiary of their kindness and generosity on many occasions.

• Charles and Sarah had a friendship like no other, beyond description with ordinary words. Their bond was/is stronger than anything imaginable and stood the test of Sarah's illness. Charles is also a teacher (high school) with summers available for travel. They went somewhere most every summer. I am forever grateful for his love and friendship, then and now.

• Dan and Sarah also had a friendship like no other. Dan *is* Gemmy Industries (which had its genesis in a rented garage prior to graduation from UD)—and if you have or have seen a Christmas or Halloween inflatable in the front yard—you have seen Gemmy. Remember Billy Bass—the singing fish plaque?? What you won't see but should know is that Sarah loved Dan and Charles with all her heart. The standing repartee was Dan asking "who do you love the best?" in front of Charles and Sarah answering "I love you best plural perfect."

- Karen (mother of six including another Sarah and Sophia, Sarah's god-daughter born December 31, 2007) lives in Atlanta. Tia Sarita was a member of her family and her five girls and one son were like Sarah's own. Karen, Deb and Sarah were UD roommates from 1979 to 1983.

- Deb and husband, John, are Rome Group members too. Sarah was Deb's maid of honor at their wedding. Add their 5 children (Lauren is also Sarah's god-daughter) and you have a peek at Sarah's extended family circle.

- Laura, Monica S. (not to be confused with Sarah's sister Monica Lynn) and Stephanie also members of the Rome Bunch were ya-ya sisterhood girlfriends who joined Sarah and Charles on many trips. How convenient that Monica S. happened to be working in New Delhi the summer Charles and Sarah traveled there before Sarah headed on to Bangkok to visit a fellow Peak Academy faculty member and his family. Her circle of life spanned continents!!

- Mary and her husband Tom are UD Alums but didn't meet Sarah until after Rome; however, as teachers they (and their 3 children) had much in common. Tia Sarita was also a member of their family.

- **1983** Three days before law school orientation, Sarah called to inform me she was *not* going to law school. No discussion, no explanation, no questions allowed. She was enrolling in another year at UD to

get her credentials as an elementary school teacher.
[As upset as I was, she was right on target. Teaching
was her passion; therefore she excelled in the
classroom and with her fellow teachers.]

- **1986** Sarah traveled to Europe solo. She visited
Charles in Austria before heading to France and
Rome. The first of many such adventures.

- Sarah was a Master Teacher. She taught fifth grade at
St. Cecelia's Catholic School immediately after
graduation, and in the Dallas Independent School
District and then in the Johnson County Kansas
(Shawnee Mission) School District. In 2004, Sarah
then returned to Dallas and taught at Peak Academy,
a DISD charter school. Some of the numerous awards
she received included: Shawnee Mission School
District Teacher of the Year nominee, Who's Who
Among American Educators, Teacher of the Year
Dallas Independent School District, Oldies '95
Teacher of the Week, WDAF Crystal Apple Nominee,
Peak Academy Teacher of the Year and Peak
Preparatory Instructional Coach of the Year. The
greatest tributes have been the many students who
supported her during her illness and attended her
wake and funeral services.

- The Kansas City network/team was chaired by
Christine (and Joe) and populated by numerous
fellow faculty and former students. Emily's comments
at Sarah's wake are included to provide a view from
the student's side of the classroom.

- Sarah and her sister, Monica, made numerous trips from Oklahoma and Texas to visit their father and stepfamily in Colorado and Minnesota. Those sister-road-trips remain mostly mysteries; however, I do know driving through western Kansas was a mandatory "everyone-stays-awake zone" enforced by music at mach-decibels.

- Sarah spent her life living for and learning from her travels usually with Charles, Monica S. Stephanie, Laura, Dan and Joe. She was serious about experiencing the world Italy, Spain, France (who can count how many times?), Germany, England, Ireland, Czech Republic, Egypt, Turkey, India, Thailand, Guatemala, Mexico and Canada. We could always expect a Christmas card picture of the most recent summer excursion.

- After round #1 of chemo-therapy in September. 2007 and before Christmas, 2007, Sarah visited Hong Kong and Beijing (with Mary, Monica S., Dan and his brother, Joe), Czech Republic, (with Laura, Monica S., Michael and Charles) New York City (with Michael, Stephanie and Charles) and Denver to visit her step-family.

- In June 2008, Sarah, her sister, Monica, and their stepfamily went to Hawaii for a family reunion and wedding. Despite increasing weakness and pain, Sarah took a helicopter tour.

Other information of interest (at least I think so) follows:

The Tattoos

Contrary to what Sarah or Monica may assert, I did *not* tell Sarah to get her first tattoo.

Sometime during the first year following her father's and stepmother's deaths, I encouraged her to do "something that would make her feel good, something that she had always wanted to do (I'm thinking a spa visit, or a new piece of art, or a new mirror for her mirror collection) but never gave herself permission because it was not practical. You cannot imagine my surprise when she (excitedly) called me to tell me she had a tattoo of an art deco man-in-the-moon on the inside of her ankle (low enough to be hidden by socks when she was in the classroom). She didn't want to experience the "tattoo-hassle" from her father. She wasn't concerned about mother because she "always supported her choices". Damned with faint praise was I.

Tattoo #2 was a compass rose (3-4" in diameter) she designed as a composite of a Norwegian map and one she had seen in Rome. A spring break trip gone awry, too much free time and some "I'll-do-anything-you-do" Kansas City friends and you get Tattoo #2 located at her sternum.

Tattoo #3 was the INF tattoo and sprang from her response to Dr. Koon, the creative genes of Peak Academy's art teacher (Lynn McClain) and the ultimate passive aggressive expression pre-chemo (along with Charles' unwavering support). We made many new friends in the chemo waiting rooms because Sarah never wore a scarf or hat.

Hum a few bars of "The Circle of Life" to begin to feel the gracious, generous, caring and supportive love of Sarah's life circle. There are hundreds in the circle and the ripples continue outward through all the students who were lucky enough to be in Miss Merdian's classroom and all those who remember her quick wit and laughing out loud with her.

Sarah was feted with a forty-eighth birthday open-house party on July 21, 2008 by the Amazing UD Bunch and Uplift/Peak Academy faculty members. In her Baylor Hobbtzelle Hospital room and the adjoining hallway, 60 + well-wishers (including Dr. Koon and his Fellow) celebrated her 48th. The celebration included a healing service conducted by Msgr. Fischer where everyone prayed:

You in me.
> *Me in You.*
>> *One Heart.*

God in me.
> *God in you.*
>> *One God.*

After she was anointed with holy oils, she thanked everyone for being there and stated:

I may not win this battle, but as long as any of you remember, I am not finished.

When Sarah left Baylor's Hobbtzelle Hospital on July 27, 2008, the ambulance attendants wheeled her down the hall which was lined, shoulder to shoulder, with all the nursing staff on duty that day. They applauded and cheered as she waved good-bye. She knew their names and their life stories. This knowing-of-names was SOP for Sarah wherever and whenever she encountered someone. Even while in pain and medicated, she still had that zest, that curiosity and yearning to encounter the new and create relationships.

On August 5, 2008, Sarah, Charles, Dan and Mary were making plans for another trip to Dan's Lake Lewisville house and an outing to a favorite midtown Dallas restaurant. She had been practicing sitting up in her wheelchair. Charles was checking out the availability of elevators and pre-ordering of menu items while Dan was making inquiry as to ambulance-like transport to the lake. The next day, Sarah began the last leg of her earth journey. At 1:30 pm, on August 7, 2008, Sarah left this life.

Each level of the cancer journey,

- the shock of the initial MMMT uterine cancer diagnosis,
- through surgery, ICU and recovery,
- the revelation of ovarian cancer,
- chemo round #1 and the belief she was in remission,
- 4 months later, the devastating realization the cancer had returned,
- facing the resulting dilemma of what to do and how to treat it,
- Chemo rounds #2 (conventional) and #3 (clinical trial)),

Sarah kept her boundless love of life, her joy of living and never, ever gave up hoping for and believing in victory. Sarah worked at Peak Academy when possible, holding on to the hope that she would be able to return to her classroom.

Sarah, my love, It was our great privilege to travel with you. Thank you for every moment you were with us.

━ ⁓

END NOTES

[1] National Cancer Institute. US National Institutes of Health. www.cancer.org.
[2] Specifically rare malignant mixed mullerian (mesodermal) tumor (mmmt) which contains both carcenomatous and sarcomatous components.
[3] CarePages—www.CarePages.com—CarePages is a free online community for patients to connect with family and friends. It is necessary to set up an account with a password. Visit "SarahMerdian" to view the messages posted and the photo gallery.

━ ⁓

CAST OF CHARACTERS

Immediate Family:
    Jane (mother)   Monica (sister)

Cousins:
    David and Loretta   Charles and Darcy

Aunts and Uncles:
    Aunt Doris (died 6-26-2008)   Aunt Joyce
    Aunt Mary   Aunt Francis
    Uncle John and Aunt Linda

The Lunsfords (aka The Mer-fords):
    Shannon and Laureen (nieces—Charis and Kaila)
    Steve and Brenda (nephew—Joseph, nieces—Alaina and
        Abigail)
    Scott and Heidi (nieces—Addision and Brooke)

Uplift/Peak—Dallas
    Winifred   Lynn
    Maria   Becky
    Graham   Rosemary
    Dawn   Teresa
    Jacqueline

Kansas—Overland Park
    Christine and Joe   Glen and Stephanie
    Linda T., her daughter, Emily T.   Linda P.
    Jessie

University of Dallas
    Charles and Michael
    Dan and Dannie (Torie, John, James)
    Mary and Tom (James, Anna, Elise)
    Karen and Mark (Adam, Sarah, Laura, Kate, Mary, Sophia)
    Deb and John (Lauren, Ryan, Luke, Brett & Gabriel)
    Steve and Pat (Geoffrey, Kimberly, Ann)
    Laura   Monica S.
    Stephanie   Mim and Chris
    John   Tom
    Mike   Mary and Mark
    Dr. Joe and Tao   Dr. Bobby
    Ed   Robert
    Bob   Thelma

Sarah's
CarePages Journal

Posted by Mary, February 5, 2007—1:32pm

January 31, 2007

Our dear friend Sarah Merdian has been diagnosed with cancer, Mixed Mesodermal Endometrial Carcinoma.

February 2, 2007

Sarah returned to Baylor for a CT Scan.

February 5, 2007

Sarah met with Dr. Koon, the Baylor oncologist, today and learned the following: "Today's meeting with the oncologist gave me more information. The situation is more complicated than I expected. Here's what I know:

During my D & C on January 22nd, a MMMT (Malignant Mixed Mesodermal tumor) was removed. Since it is a "mixed" cancer, it spreads. If it has spread then chemo and radiation will be required. Friday's CT scan showed enlarged ovaries. This could be from the spreading, an independent tumor, or it could possibly be benign. They won't know until the pathology results are returned. The scan also showed two herniated areas along both sides of my abdominal wall that will need to be addressed.

Scar tissue from my previous abdominal surgeries (1993, 1994, and 2003) will make this surgery very difficult. There is a strong chance that I will need some bowel re-sectioning as well.

My surgery, no final date yet, but probably around the 15th will be exploratory as well as to remove the uterus, tubes, and ovaries. They will be removing the bulk of the disease. They will do biopsies of lymph areas. My hospital stay will probably be at least a week. It is possible that I will need to be in ICU for a couple days after surgery. A six week recovery period is still expected, and then will be adjusted if chemo/radiation is planned.

Oh, the good news is that there is no way that the incision will distort any tattoos. Also, my doctor was "doing a favor" in surgery today for the very doctor that he wants to assist for the bowel portion. Dr. Koon said, "So, really, your timing is perfect." Thank heavens for small victories. I'll take them."

***

February 5, 2007—7:45pm

Sarah receives a call from Dr. Koon, He wants to do a biopsy of her ovary. This procedure will be done later this week by a radiologist. If the biopsy shows cancer, then they will NOT do the surgery, but rather start chemotherapy. If the biopsy is benign, then they will go ahead with the surgery on Thursday, February 15th.

***

February 6, 2007

In true Sarah fashion, she follows up with the latest update:

I can't believe I forgot to mention that as I enter the doctors' office yesterday, I see a GEMMY INDUSTRIES Dancing Hamster sitting on the check-in counter. Charles says it must be a sign, and I said, "Now I'm really scared." Certainly my uterus can't be replaced with a mini snow globe, right?

God Bless Sarah...Keep the faith!

———〜〜———

February 6, 2007—10:55pm

Due to the fact that I've been taking a low dose 81mg aspirin for heart health, the "pelvic mass" biopsy cannot be performed before Monday due the risk of bleeding. The biopsy results will take a few days and it is very possible that the surgery will need to be re-scheduled. Nothing is constant but change.

Charles pointed out that a positive note to this change might be that I would get to spend Valentine's Day doing something other than "a bowel prep". I love that guy.

I'm so thankful for all of the thoughts and prayers.

Sarah

———〜〜———

February 7, 2007—9:44am

Since the biopsy results will take a few days, the new(est) date for surgery (if needed) will be February 19th or 20th. The best news is that the doctor said it was okay for me to get a new tattoo this weekend. Every dark cloud...

———〜〜———

February 7, 2007—8:35pm

Today I visited the cardiologist. (Dr. High...really) After doing an EKG, interview and exam, she said that I fell into the low-risk category (yeah for swimming) and that I was cleared for surgery. (now scheduled for Monday, February 19th at 7:15 am)

I was able to get a relaxing massage this afternoon. However, by the time I got home, Dr. High's office had called and now wants to schedule a non-stress echocardiogram. Not sure what part of "non-stress" that call wants to be, and I believe my parking fees alone are paying for the new wing at Baylor. I did, however, appreciate Dr. High's parting comment today. *"Sometimes we open the door to fear, and nothing is there."*

I can't tell you all how comforting your thoughts and prayers are to me. Where would I be without such love and support?

Sarah

February 9, 2007—7:03pm

I saw Dr. High today after the echocardiogram, and she said, *"Sarah, you're blessed with a beautiful heart."* I know I'm blessed in so many ways. Something is happening that I didn't foresee. I feel really at peace with the person that I am. Who knew?

I told my class about the cancer today. They were champs, and I'm lucky to have such wonderful support at school. In fact, Lynn, our resident artist, has designed great tattoo for my head. I'll be sure to post a photo. Thank goodness for such delights.

I hope everyone has a great weekend. Please know that I visit this page all the time, and reread your messages. They're a great source of laughter and comfort.

Love, Sarah

February 12, 2007—6:16am

Well, this morning I'm heading over to the hospital to have the "pelvic mass" biopsy done. I'll be there most of the day. However, the most exciting news is the new tattoo. I'm thinking that there is NO WAY that the biopsy hurts more than the tattoo.

Lynn McClain, our resident artist at Peak, came up with the design. It's the letters I.N.F. which, of course, stands for I'M NOT

FINISHED...because I'm not. One of my options might be chemotherapy, and I have thought that a scalp tattoo would be an empowering statement on a bald head, and here we are.

Thanks so much to Charles for the haircut. Thanks to Mike and the folks at Obscurities, and thanks to all of you.

Love, Sarah

～～

February 12, 2007—4:37pm

I'm back home from the biopsy. It was more than I expected.

Dr. Martin, my resident, (for you Grey's Anatomy fans, more of a McSereney) was patient and calming. He explained that my ovarian cyst is about the size of a grapefruit, and they would be trying to take tissue samples during the biopsy. The pathologist, Dr. Laurie, (for you House fans, I guess), would check the samples to see if they would even be viable for diagnosis. (and she would also hold my legs down during part of the procedure.) There is no guarantee that a diagnosis will be possible from these samples, but they will try their best.

They did an ultrasound to locate the mass, and marked my abdomen. I got a stingy shot of lidocaine, and then they did four biopsy samples. I was unprepared for the incredible pressure and the sensation of the needle going into different body parts. In fact, I was somewhat worried that they might be coming out of my back.

It was one of those automatic crying—sort of a faucet— situations. (Who knew your ears could fill up with tears?) It was the pressure, rather than pain, that was so upsetting.

But I am thankful for many things.

1. It's over.
2. It's so much less invasive than an exploratory surgery
3. My care providers were top-notch.

4. When I heard that I was going to have to have the fourth sample taken, I panicked inside, and I simply didn't think I would be able to do it. That inner well that held the ability to be still and go through it once more was completely empty. And I asked for strength, and I got it, and it didn't come from me. It just came through me.

The pathology report will be sent to Dr. Koon later this week, and then we'll go from there.

Your unwavering support is making such a difference for me. I'm blessed, and I ask you to continue your prayers for strength. I know this is just the beginning.

Love, Sarah

February 14, 2007—6:19am

Happy Valentine's Day everyone! I'm still waiting to hear test results and other info from the doctor. This is certainly an exercise in patience and letting go.

Yours 'til the Hersheys kiss,

Sarah

February 15, 2007—5:12pm

Today Sarah met with Dr. Koon and the news wasn't good. The biopsy report showed that the cancer has spread to the ovaries. There are two choices for treatment. One is to have chemo to slow the growth of the cancer, which wouldn't cure it, but it would help prolong life. Surgery would be a more aggressive treatment plan, but would not cure the disease either and due to the three previous abdominal surgeries, this surgery would be complicated and risky.

Sarah is unwilling to accept the prognosis for a two year life expectancy and is pursuing a second opinion. Dan and Dannie Flaherty are helping Sarah to set up an appointment at M.D. Anderson in Houston to pursue treatment alternatives. Please continue to keep Sarah in your prayers. She so appreciates all the messages, wishes, and prayers.

———————

February 17, 2007—10:31am
Some beautiful things are happening for me.

- A parent at school conspired (collaborated) with the art teacher to create buttons with my tattoo I.N.F. logo. Imagine standing at the door of the classroom as my whole class walks in wearing them. *"We're wearing these to support you, Miss Merdian."* Yes, I stood there and bawled. (Charles is already planning the nationwide marketing program for these pins. Watch out Lance Livestrong)
- I spent a great evening at Club Schmitz with the Flahertys and surprise guests Sarah and Laura Papania. Schmitz will never be a place to wallow in anything that doesn't come in a bottle.
- Dan and Dannie's efforts have started a big ball rolling at M.D. Anderson and my mother has even ousted the cat from the guest room in Houston. After a draining volley of phone tag, my records have been faxed, my films are in my possession, and the slides are being FedEx-ed on Monday. I'll hear from them on Tuesday.
- Katy Sauser has agreed to substitute in my class, and I am so happy to hand my cupcakes over to such safe

hands. They take their first big state test on Tuesday, and say a little prayer for them because this has been hard on them too. They've worked so hard and come so far, and I want them to be able to focus and show all that they know.

- And probably the funniest moment of the past few days was when Dan brought over a few Gemmy products for motivation and support. One was a Dancing Hamster that sings "I Will Survive" (nothing says hope for the cure like disco favorites), but the moment was made perfect when Dan pushed the ON button and

........nothing
........nothing
........nothing
........happened.

"I swear it was working at the office!" and he proceeds in that tender supportive caring way to smack the bottom of the hamster repeatedly and beat its head on the table. (Really, I can't make this stuff up. It's priceless.) After the (sorry PETA) hamster mauling, he set it on the table, and yes, it did finally work. It's always nice to witness a metaphor for letting go.

I am surrounded by love and support and prayers. In fact, I have this mental image of God saying, "Okay, it's about HER again." Please understand that I'm a little slow on returning calls, and I will probably need to get some sort of headset to offset the cauliflower ear and overdeveloped "hold the phone up" arm muscles and/or permanent neck crick. I so appreciate hearing from so many dear friends, family, and students. Your support means so much.

Love, Sarah

  Sarah Merdian

February 18, 2007—11:26pm

Today my path led me to the chapel at the University of Dallas, and I found the following from the Wisdom of Solomon (6:12) "Wisdom is radiant and unfading, and she is easily discerned by those who love her, and is found by those who seek her."

I certainly do not possess the wisdom to understand the meaning or purpose of this cancer. Something wonderful must come from it. Why else would it exist? In this quest, I am also not finished.

So many of you have sent forth an outpouring of love and support, and I'm asked over and over what can be done for me. I have a few ideas.

- Support me by being a support for each other. Everyone reading this has been touched by this cancer. We all feel a certain sense of powerlessness which is frustrating and difficult. (and I've never read such a roster of strong-willed individuals in my life.)
- Get whatever you've been avoiding to have checked, checked by your doctor. Let's not allow fear to replace our search for wisdom and understanding. Illness does not have to be discussed in whispers. It's harder to fight an invisible dragon.
- Allow yourself the grace to be okay with whom you are and where you are. I've spent most of my life fretting and regretting my body, and now I realize that it's truly a treasure that is worth the fight.
- Laugh (what if it really is the best medicine?), and feel free to laugh at my cancer, too. I do, every single day. If I'm not playing the C card, I'm trying to figure out a way to do it.

The good folks at M.D. Anderson will get my information on Tuesday, and a couple other resources have been sent my way as well. This week will bring new roads to travel. I love hearing from all of you. I read your messages over and over. Sorrow shared is sorrow divided. I continue to seek understanding and strength, and I appreciate all of your support.

Love, Sarah

PS I had a glorious weekend (well, except for the cancer, of course).

❖

February 19, 2007—11:47pm

Something from the "WHAT NOT TO SAY" collection.

A friend at school has been helping me do the paperwork to get my Baylor Health Club membership account frozen for a couple months since I'm not swimming right now. (Don't worry, Baylor will still be getting that money somewhere else), and it turns out that I needed a form faxed by the doctor. So I left a message for the doctor and today I got a call from the fitness center.

The girl is confused because on my paperwork, it states that I want to freeze my account for two months, but the doctor's letter says that I'm terminal. So, she wants to know if I really want to freeze or just terminate the membership. I suggested that we try the two month freeze and I'd get back to her if I needed to change the status.

I've laughed all day.

…And something from the MYSTERIOUS WAYS collection. I decide that I need to find a place to get a facial. The few times I've had one, I've been able to drift away to some happy place and emerge glowing both inside and outside. Turns out quite a few salons are closed on Monday, but I find one on the internet that even has a facial/massage combo special on Mondays, and yes they can fit me in today. Well, the facial was mediocre, but oh, my massage!

Arturo, the massage therapist, used to be a nurse, and when he read about the cancer on my forms, he wanted to talk to me about it. He was concerned that a traditional massage, which stimulates the lymphatic system, might not be beneficial since we're uncertain about the spreading of the cancer. Instead, he'd like to use reflexology and pressure to help me relax and start to heal.

What a gentle and wonderful man. The entire experience was completely calming. He asked me how I was feeling about the cancer and shared a few thoughts.

- The weight of our troubles often makes us look at the ground, but the stars are above. We should be looking there because there's so much more to see.
- Remember that we've been given a perfect, perfect body. Sometimes we find help on the outside and sometimes it is within.
- Laughter creates endorphins which will help you with pain. So will prayer.
- When you are scared, recall the wonderful moments of your life. Fear keeps us from healing, but happiness helps us heal.

I told Arturo that I was lucky to meet him today, and he told me that he wasn't scheduled for today, but they had just called him in. Wow.

Thanks to all of you for the laughs and the prayers and all of those wonderful moments that continue to be enjoyed. I think I might hear something from M.D. Anderson tomorrow. They will receive my pathology slides in the morning.

Yours with a terminal grin,

Sarah

———

February 21, 2007—11:51am

Might I suggest trying to make a flowchart to follow this? (Funny, but the past two weeks feel exactly this way.)

Charles' brother-in-law, Gerry Jacob, has a friend (Dr. Rob Coleman) who is an MD Anderson gynecological oncologist (which is referred to as Gyn-Onc and, I believe, is pronounced JIN-ANKH, which brings to mind either a Star Wars creature or a Milton-Bradley strategy game from the 1970s AND might be the secret lyrics to the Pink Panther theme. Really try it out. It works).

Anyway, Dan gets the doctor's number from Gerry and I talk to Dr. Coleman this morning. He's a nice guy, and he mainly agrees with the treatment ideas from Baylor, but has a few suggestions to consider (such as a chemo-surgery-chemo plan?). He tells me to continue with my pursuit to get into MDA, and maybe we can touch base later.

About 15 minutes later, Denise (originally from NY, but now in Houston....doesn't miss the cold weather) from MDA calls and they have an appointment for me on March 1st. She goes through all of the necessary paperwork info, directions, etc. and at the end of the conversation mentions; btw, the appointment is with a Dr. Coleman. Weird.

Since then, Dannie has spoken to Liz, Dr. Coleman's assistant, and perhaps the appointment can be bumped up. The March 1st date is, in fact, a quick turn around. It's nice to have a point of reference now, and we'll go from here.

The only other news is that I decided to get my hair cut yesterday. After seeing my hospital bed-head after my outpatient treatments, I thought a cut might be considered community service for the hospital staff. All I can say is. think k.d.lang. Well, I have the shoes to match.

I am feeling okay physically, but this has been very draining emotionally. I'm finding nap times during the day and trying to get a little recharged. I hear my class is doing well, and I'm thankful for that.

Thanks too for all the support. It means so much,

Love, Sarah
(a/k/a Shorty von Haircut)

February 22, 2007—8:52am

Yesterday I got a call from LifeMasters Support. They have been contracted through Blue Cross Blue Shield to reach out to me. According to their website: "Since its founding, LifeMasters has been focused on one mission: to empower individuals living with chronic diseases to achieve optimal health."

The lady explains that she will take some baseline information from me at this time, then I will be contacted periodically be a nurse to help me with my disease. They offer support in areas of pain management, lifestyle, and emotional need. You know, from where I'm sitting, I think, WHY NOT? Why not take advantage of every bit of support offered to me?

She proceeds to ask questions about my health history and wants to address any back pain both past and present. Well, in 1994 I did pull a muscle that had me flat on my back for three days, but since then, I've been pretty good. She wants me to rate my current back pain on the 0 to 10 scale. (I say 0). She wants to know if my back pain keeps me from doing things like cooking or walking.

Now, I'm not the sharpest knife in the drawer, (or do I now get to say I'm not the most malignant tumor in the uterus?) but I'm cluing in that she thinks back pain is my big ISSUE.

So I ask her...Do you have anything about cancer on that list?

    LM Why no, why?

    SMM Well, I don't have any back pain. I have been diagnosed with cancer.

    LM No, there's nothing about cancer on my paperwork. Let me check. ......um....no...but I do have one more question.......Are you experiencing any depression or difficulty sleeping?

    SMM Yes, but it is due to the cancer NOT back pain.

    LM Oh, that makes sense. Well, that's all I have for you today.

    A nurse will be contacting you later in the week.

SMM about the cancer?

LM No, but you should tell her about that. I hope everything turns out okay for you.

So, of course I'm reminded of the old "Who's on First" routine (and my personal rendition with a hotel concierge in Mexico wondering why my deceased father has not checked in to the hotel yet.)

I'm laughing,

I'm laughing.

Yours 'til life masters support,

Sarah

—~—

February 23, 2007 8:30am

Last evening, Dr. Koon called me at home. He hadn't heard from me, so he wanted to check how I was doing. He wanted to make sure that I hadn't decided to go home, "and do nothing."

I had mistakenly assumed that since his office sent my files to MDA that he would be notified. I mentioned that my new doctor, Dr. Rob Coleman, had mentioned knowing Dr. Koon. Yes, and Dr. Koon thinks I am in good hands. *"Rob has a breadth of knowledge in chemotherapy and is a talented surgeon."* We ended our conversation with his reassurance that seeking a second opinion is a good idea and that no matter what course of treatment I select, he would like to be kept in the loop on my progress. What a nice guy.

That was my second home phone call from Dr. Koon. My massage therapist also called me at home to check up on me this week. I seem to be surrounded by such caring people.

Piglet sidled up to Pooh from behind,
"Pooh!," **he whispered.**
"Yes, Piglet?"

"Nothing," said Piglet, taking Pooh's paw. *"I just wanted to be sure of you."*

Have a great weekend, everyone,

Sarah

⌒⌒

February 24, 2007—9:19am

Yesterday I had the pleasure of meeting with Monsignor Don Fischer (you know, my spiritual advisor and domestic ambient lighting director). Don was our chaplain at UD (University of Dallas) during college, and it's been a joy to keep in touch with him since then. As always, his insight and direction were clear and comforting. Plus, we always find something to laugh about. I feel that I am in a better place after talking with Don, and I look forward to many more conversations in the future

As it stands now, Dannie will fly down to Houston with me on Wednesday afternoon and help me through my orientation at M.D. Anderson. I'm grateful to have a seasoned survivor by my side. (Yes, seasoned means experienced, not OLD).

I'm not certain how long this first stage of appointments and testing will take, but I'll be staying at my mother's house during this time. There's even a hint that Charles might find his way down to Houston over the weekend.

I'll have computer access, so I hope to continue hearing from all of you. This page has been such a comfort and support for me. (Thanks again for setting this up, Mim!)

I continue to find many reasons for laughter each day (many on this page!), and I'm also enjoying Norah Jones' new cd. (It's a keeper.)

Have a great weekend.

Love, Sarah

⌒⌒

February 25, 2007—10:48am

> *All truths are easy to understand once they are*
> *discovered; the point is to discover them.*
> —Galileo Galilei

What I'm discovering....

- Cancer can be a window rather than a wall.
- Light comes from sources you never imagined.
- You can laugh in the face of anything.
- Fear paralyzes. Love trumps fear.
- None of us are finished.

Yours 'til Houston's got a problem,

Sarah

———

February 26, 2007—9:35am

A couple of weeks ago (or has it been forever), when I first entered the Sammons Cancer Center at Baylor, I happened to notice the big gift shop "Appearance Center" in the main lobby. The store carries all sorts of things. Post-surgery bras, hats, wigs, watercolors with religious verses, and yes.....jewelry!

I didn't really go in and shop. I guess I felt that same, "this isn't really my store" feeling like I have outside a sporting goods store or a Victoria's Secret, but I did do a little window shopping. Now, there must be 20 wigs on different mannequins, but one (it's on the top row of the upper left, if you go) is so disturbing.

The wig is fine, but the mannequin's neck is like four times longer than humanly possible. I mean more than those tribal ladies with the neck rings. I mean, giraffe-ishly unnatural. On subsequent visits, I couldn't decide which was worse. Sitting in a chair facing the glass, or having my back to her knowing she was peering down upon me.

Now, it's funny where your mind goes in a cancer ward waiting room, but I've realized—especially since the haircut—that Girafferella and I share something. The need for dangling earrings. Yep, I've yet to find the place to register for cancer gifts, (seems weddings and babies get all the good registries), but be on the look out for cute dangling earrings. It's called jewelry therapy, and we all have heard of it. It's probably even tax deductible.

Remember, I'm more of a silver than a gold, and I love stones, beads, wires, hoops, filigree, cloisonné, precious and semi-precious gems, and thanks to Charles, I'm even rediscovering the beauty of posts. I've even taken to wearing pairs. Yes, it's all part of the journey. Stay tuned, because I'm currently researching chocolate therapy.

Yours 'til the ear rings, Dangley von Loberton

February 28, 2007—1:22am

Hey, there's a rumor going around that my class might get on this page on Wednesday. If they get to try it out, please remember the following.

- Be sure to sign your name after your entry. (I'd love to see a great closing and your name)
- Be CERTAIN to spell all word wall words correctly. The Your/You're and too/to/two sets are toughies.
- Try to include at least one positive thing in your message; maybe a connection, idea, observation, info from a project, etc. Remember a fun time, like when the math problem was so hot and spicy that it actually MELTED the pen!
- Use your great word choice, metaphors, similes, and voice in your messages.

- I know you ALL miss my singing. Please stop crying. Dry your tears. Repair the windows.
- Lots of people get to see this page, so remember that we tell others that school is "hard", Miss Merdian is "mean" and all we do is work, work, work and never smile. That will help protect my reputation.
- Since I'm going to the MDA Medical Center, I want to try out some new group names. Check them out.

Medicinal Monday,
Testing Tuesday
Waiting Room Wednesday
Thermometer Thursday
Feverish Friday

I'd love to hear your suggestions.
I'm looking forward to getting your messages.
Yours 'til Houston Rockets,

Miss Merdian

March 01, 2007—09:48pm

The Gynecology Oncology waiting room at M. D. Anderson is huge. Comfortable chairs are placed throughout a big bright open room. When it's your turn to go for paperwork or examination, a nurse comes out, walks around, and calls your name. "Sarah Merdian......Miss Merdian....Sarah Merdian" Imagine the irony of sitting in the cancer waiting room and hearing this patient's name being called......."Miss Fortune.........Miss Fortune" I'm thinking we could all raise our hands. However, I am back home tonight, and I am feeling good about the visit.

Today's visit to M. D. Anderson can be summed up by one word: ENCOURAGING.

I met Dr. Rob Coleman and his teaching fellow Dr. Solomon (who Dannie did not completely insult by calling her a "trainee") in Houston today. Here's the scoop.

- They agree with the diagnosis from Baylor. It's a MMMT that is also present in the ovaries.
- Surgery seems to be their first choice for treatment. Right now, they need to completely assess the risk factors for such a surgery.
- They had some other tests done today blood, x-ray, EKG, etc. and I will go back to Houston to meet with an internist next Wednesday.
- I will meet with Dr. Coleman and the complete team next Thursday. He will have had time to review all of my films and get the results from the internist as well as from today's tests.

I really got the VIP treatment today. Dr. Coleman put us of all at ease. He seems genuine, positive and caring, and I felt comfortable there immediately. It was also a great idea to have my posse there at the appointment. (Thanks Mother and Dannie).

As we left Mother's this morning, it was dreary and beginning to rain. By this afternoon, it was a beautiful sunny day. The weather mirrored my spirits exactly, and I have never felt more positive and hopeful.

Yours 'til Little Miss Sun-shines,

Sarah

March 06, 2007—11:20pm

So Be It. Since my return to Dallas, I've been trying to fight a respiratory infection that resulted from seasonal allergies and a cat visit. I've been coughing so much that my teeth even ache, and in the back of my mind I've kept saying. "Hurry up! Hurry up! Get better so they can do surgery! If you can't conquer cat, how can you hope to conquer cancer!"

Well, I'm trying to remember to embrace this body I have rather than fight against it.

If I look at it another way, I realize..... Hey! I'm heading down to see an expert in internal medicine tomorrow afternoon. How perfect, because I really need someone's expertise. Laura Daly used to say, "My very best thinking has gotten me to this point." and now.....so be it. The expert can step in.

I need to remind and realize that illness is a condition, not an accusation or shortcoming, or punishment. It is what is it is. So be it.

Some of my class are trying to keep my mind sharp with some poetic riddles. A few need a nudge or two back on track. I know my friends at Peak will assist with that. With me, it always takes a village (or two). I'll keep you posted from Houston.

Yours 'til the cough drops,

Miss M. (a/k/a Sarah)

⌐⌐

March 07, 2007—5:05pm

After a wonderful Peak Parent (Thanks Sandy!) dropped me off at Love Field, I made it to the gate to sit and wait and cough. As I'm throwing away a tissue, a woman (who if you're a LOST fan, resembles Rousseau same crazy hair and eyes just a little bit shorter.) tells me that she has a note for me. The note reads:

My name is Helen. You have beautiful hands (like a pianist, she later tells me) and I'm sure you are beautiful on the inside. Would you consider having surgery? It may save your life?

I ask her, *"What kind of surgery?"* and her response is, *"Well, something that would make you SMALLER."*

  Sarah Merdian

Yes, I cannot make this up. Here's what happens next:

SM—Well, Helen. Funny, but I'm getting on this plane to see if I'm going to have surgery for my CANCER.

Helen—Both of my parents had cancer. I'm just waiting for my turn.

SM—Maybe it won't come your way.

Helen—You probably hate me now.

SM—No, I just think that you need to remember that you are seeing a snapshot of my life and that you don't know me. You don't know what I've been through or what I'm going through.

Helen—You're right. I'm so sorry. I shouldn't have said anything. We're going to Sheryl Crow's concert tonight and we're all wearing pink shirts. I know you hate me.

SM—Please don't let this ruin your day.

Helen—Let's get on the plane. I've learned so much from you today. I'm 50 years old and I've learned a life lesson. I have been enlightened. Do you want to sit together on the plane?

SM—No, I think I'm going to sit by myself and relax.

AHHHHHH!

As for my doctor's appointment today. It's all good. Dr. Sahai said that I am cleared for surgery, and I've been given a beta blocker to help with my blood pressure. I'm supposed to take some more OTC meds for the respiratory stuff, but it's not going to affect a surgery date. I see the anesthesiologist tomorrow morning and then Dr. Coleman at noon. I'll keep you posted.

Yours 'til Helen's a hand basket,

Sarah

March 08, 2007—4:52pm

I just got back from Houston (no airport drama) after meeting with Dr. Coleman today. Here's the scoop

- We have a tentative surgery date. Wednesday, March 21st at high noon. We're waiting to see if the plastics surgeon is available on that day.
- I will probably go back to Houston next week to meet with anesthesia and plastics.
- I'm trying my best to get over this horrid allergen-triggered asthma attack. The surgery date gives me about two weeks to regain some strength.
- Dr. Coleman attended a Gyn Onc conference in San Diego this weekend and saw Dr. Koon. They talked about my case while standing on the flight deck of an aircraft carrier (like you do.)
- My hospital stay will probably be about a week, maybe a day or two in ICU. It's a major surgery (but it will be easiest for me. I'll be asleep.)
- Before Dr. Coleman left, he walked around the table to give me a hug. What's not to love about this guy?
- Thanks to the Bartas for letting me stay at their place. Mother got the fun of traveling around with me coughing continuously.

Here's a link to something fun. It's nice to know that everyone is behind me (even Homer). Just click play after the file downloads. There are two different tracks. (yes, I was called Merd in college.) You have to copy and paste.

http://web.mac.com/doctorchang/iWeb/Site/Download Page.html

Thanks to everyone for the groovy earrings. I've gotten tons of compliments and they certainly deflect from the hair.

Yours 'til the surgeon's general,

Sarah

March 14, 2007—10:22am

Happy Spring Break! I'm still waiting to hear more from MDA. I have spoken to them every day, and they're trying to coordinate schedules. I guess I'm being given a wonderful opportunity to practice my life skill of PATIENCE. (The patient patient?) As far as I know, the surgery is still next Wednesday.

The cough is better, but still not gone. I've gotten a lot more rest, and the best news is that the I.N.F. pins (thanks Rosemary M.) are on their way to Colorado, Tulsa, Kansas City, and Houston. As always, I appreciate your support.

Yours 'til seven days of waiting doesn't make one weak,

Sarah

March 17, 2007—11:19am

> *A good laugh and a long sleep are the best cures in the doctor's book.*   **—Irish proverb**

HAPPY ST. PATRICK'S DAY! I've spoke to MDA every day this week, and still, we're not definite on my schedule for surgery. I expect to hear more finalized details on Monday.

My cough has caused a more severe muscle strain, but it only hurts when I laugh, cough, or breathe. I'm not feeling too strong these days, but I figure it's good practice for what's coming up.

I really enjoy hearing from everyone. It brightens my day in so many ways. I'm hanging in there.

Yours 'til the sham rocks,

Sarah O'Merdian

⁓

March 19, 2007—03:47pm

> *Change is inevitable except from a vending machine.* —Robert C. Gallagher

Well, I've heard from Dr. Han, Dr. Coleman's Fellow, and here's the latest. I will go down to Houston on Friday, 3/23, to meet with Dr. Butler, the plastic surgeon, and anesthesia. My surgery will be on Monday, March 26th.

The good news is that I have a week to get completely better and head into surgery feeling strong and well-rested. The cough is fading, the side is mending, and the mind is almost clearing.

Thanks for keeping me in your thoughts and prayers.

Yours 'til I'm in stitches,

Sarah

⁓

March 21, 2007—1:40pm

Several people have mentioned that they don't exactly know what surgical procedure is planned for next Monday. Here's what I know:

> Dr. Coleman is planning to do a total (complete) hysterectomy, which is removal of the uterus and cervix, and he is also planning on removing my tubes and ovaries which I have discovered is called

a salpingo-oophorectomy. (Now, I'm sure we're all thinking that "salpingo" sounds like some exotic dish as in "I'll have the chicken salpingo with the couscous medium spicy, please", and I can't even put my head around a surgical procedure that begins with OOP. It's bad enough when you hear your hair stylist or nail tech say "Oops!" I can't imagine hearing that in the O.R. Maybe that's another good reason for anesthesia.)

Dr. Coleman (and friends) will also do "staging" which is taking tissue samples for pathology to see if and where the cancer has spread. This information will affect the chemo and radiation plans. It takes over a week to get all of the info from pathology.

Dr. Butler, the plastic surgeon, will be "opening and closing" (sounds very Broadway play to me) and he will also address the herniated areas on either side of my abdomen. I meet with Dr. Butler on Friday, and I'm sure we will discuss swimsuit options at that time as well.

The surgery is scheduled for 7:30 am on Monday morning. Since I've been sleeping in until nearly 10:00 lately, this will be an effort for me. Luckily, I get to go right back to sleep. (Again, I love anesthesia).

It is a possibility that I will be in ICU for a day or so, and then I'm expecting about a week stay in the hospital. Since I'll be on morphine, I've been pleading with the powers that be that NO sound activated Gemmy items find their way down to Houston. All I can say is that last time there were some scary hallucinations. Not fun. Not helpful. Not kidding.

I will probably stay in Houston another week after I am released from the hospital. I'm armed with puzzle books, seasons 1 and 3 of 24 (anyone have a season two on DVD?), Prisonbreak, books, my ipod, angels, a rosary, symbala, St. Peregrine medal, prayer shawl, and enough cute earrings to change with every IV replacement.

I also feel surrounded by your positive energy, support, love, and prayers. I think I'm good to go.

Yours 'til OOP, there it is,

Sarah

March 23, 2007—8:42pm

Greetings from Houston.

Today's meetings with Dr. Butler and Anesthesiology went well AND were very different than what I expected. The most surprising news came from anesthesia. After looking at my echocardiogram report, the doctor informed me the rating of 60 in some systolic portion put me in the ATHLETE category for the heart. She said that she was only a 50 or 55 and that my swimming has really paid off. That's right. ATHLETE. I don't know if the Nike people will be calling, but I guess I won't be surprised. All in all, anesthesia thinks I'm good to go.

Now, the Plastic Surgery department was another story. I should have been tipped off by the photographer's lighting equipment in the examination room, but maybe I haven't watched enough episodes of Nip/Tuck to be in the know. Let's just say that I did not expect to be drawn on with marker (black and purple) and end up standing naked against a blue wall in front of a team of four while someone took pictures. Turn left, turn right, face the corner, hands behind your butt. I asked if I should smile but they swear my face won't be in any of the photos.

The Papania girls gave me a set of precious sharpies for recovery fun this week, but Dr. Butler gave me an INDUSTRIAL SHARPIE (yes, it's called that) and I'm instructed to trace over his lines on my body before I shower this weekend. Surreal.

It seems like I will be having two surgeries at once. The plastics team will be removing a lot of scar tissue (no more belly button-really) and addressing my weakened abdominal muscle issues. They will repair the herniated areas and try to remove some fat and skin that cause stress on the area. Oh........and then there's the hysterectomy and cancer portion of the ride.

I will have "more drains that you can count" and will probably have to have some type of battery-operated VAC wound dressing for weeks after the surgery. The procedures and protocols seem state-of-the-art here, and despite a somewhat overwhelming description by Dr. Butler, I feel like I am in the best possible hands.

Thanks to Dannie for working wonders to get me a room at the adjoining hotel for the night prior to the operation. I have to check in at the hospital at 5:15am and the surgery is set for 7:30. Charles is heading down on Saturday, and I'm hoping for a somewhat relaxing (is that possible) weekend. Thanks for surrounding me with such care and support.

Yours 'til the belly buttons,

Sarah

PS—I'm including a few more "enhanced" versions of our family picture just because I think it's so funny.

PS—To answer my sister's question. Some people say they are wearing the INF (I'm Not Finished) pins in support of a cancer patient but I guess "I'm wearing this pin because the scary lady at work told me to do it" is equally supportive and helpful.

March 26, 2007—12:27pm

Sarah's mom, Jane, called and said the operation is going well and Sarah's vital signs are good. Dr. Butler finished stage 1 of the operation around 10:30am... (surgery started at 8:01 a.m.)

Dr. Coleman is still operating. They expect to finish around 2 p.m. today.

Keep praying! Mary

—◦—

March 26, 2007—3:29pm

Sarah is still in surgery. It is taking a bit longer than expected. Jane is hoping for an update at 4:00 p.m.

Mary

—◦—

March 26, 2007—5:37pm

Dr. Coleman spoke with Jane and told her that he finished removing the ovarian mass, tubes, ovaries and uterus. Unfortunately, there was also some visible cancer in the lower abdominal lymph nodes. He will know more after pathology. Dr. Butler took care of 3 hernias, removed scar tissue and is still reconstructing the abdominal wall. He hopes to finish in a couple of hours.

Stay strong, Sarah!

Mary

—◦—

March 26, 2007—9:45pm

Sarah is finally out of the marathon surgery. Thank God! She is in ICU and resting. The doctor thinks she will be in the hospital for at least 2 weeks. More details tomorrow.

xoxo Mary

—◦—

March 27, 2007—7:58am

Jane called to say that Sarah had an ok night. They are giving her an epidural to help with the pain and to enable her to be ambulatory.

If she can get up and move around it helps reduce the risk of blood clots. They are hoping to remove the breathing tube today. If you are checking this page for updates, please consider leaving Sarah a message. She enjoys reading and rereading your comments.

Thanks, Mary

❧

March 27, 2007—3:41pm

Sarah's mother just called with the following update:

- The breathing tube has been removed. Sarah is breathing on her own with the help of supplemental oxygen.
- Although there is much pain, which was to be expected, the epidural for pain management has been administered and is helping.
- Sarah is sitting up on the side of the bed, and they hope to have her up and moving about as the day progresses.

A number of friends have asked about sending flowers, gifts or visiting. At this time we don't know how long Sarah will be in ICU where visitation is limited and flowers are prohibited. No doubt the minute Sarah is transferred to a patient room she will be hunting for a computer to check this page and resume communicating with her dear friends and loved ones.

Please continue to keep Sarah in your prayers *Mim*

❧

March 27, 2007—12:23pm

The following email update comes to us from Sarah's mother at 10:10 am this morning:

Sarah is in ICU after yesterday's marathon 12+ hrs
surgery. Both Doctors are pleased with results.
Major issues with abdominal repair, restoration
and reconstruction. Cancer well within the
abdominal cavity complete hysterectomy along
with other nodules and masses/cysts. "removed
everything I could see"   —*Dr. Coleman.*
Chemo for sure. Hospital stay probably 2 weeks.

Thank you for the family that stayed with me yesterday and for the
family that supported us with prayers and positives vibes. Keep it coming!
Sarah's color is excellent and she is writing letters on my palm
to communicate until they remove the breathing tube (any minute
now). You will love this she told a med tech to get me a chair!!
Mother Merdian

Keep the prayers flowing *Mim*

March 27, 2007—6:00pm
And a final update of the day from Mother Merdian, she writes:

Sarah has been sitting up in the "pink chair"
(don't think cushions) for about 25 to 30 minutes.
Big milestone along with breathing solo. Epidural
meds are big assist in dealing with the pain. No
food or water but she does get to swab her mouth
out with a tiny piece of green sponge on a stick.
Even if you try to think lime Popsicle—it just
doesn't compute. Please pray for a peaceful night
and restoring rest.
Mother Merdian

March 28, 2007—1:35pm

Today's mid-day update comes from Mother Merdian:

—First part of last night was pretty good. Not so after 1 pm. Pain meds adjusted again. She has received a blood transfusion this morning. I would describe her as "restless" as she tried to cope with the pain. No word on whether we can leave ICU today. Stay tuned, keep the candles lighted and the prayers coming.

Mother Merdian

❦

March 28, 2007—4:39pm

Good News from Mother Merdian:

—As soon as the patient room (# G-1082) is cleaned, Sarah is moving to Room G-1082. Hooray!!! Don't know exact time, but should be today!!
—Sarah is coping with the pain much better since the last adjustment to the med formula.

❦

March 29, 2007—3:59pm

Today's update from Houston:

—Sarah is on liquids today first thing she asked for was A Diet Coke. She is walking as I type this!!!!
—Pain management program is working—she is getting some rest.
—She feels well enough to give me instructions on how to arrange everything in her room— especially her little bedside table. I am also accused of hovering—I am and I will. It is in the

fine print of Motherhood that I can. Keep those prayers and good vibes coming—we are MARCHING FORWARD!

Mother Merdian

March 30, 2007—10:06am

TGIF with positive news from Mother Merdian:

—Good news!! Sarah gets solid (but bland) food today. Pain still under "control" and she will walk and sit up in the chair again today.
—Dr. Butler said he is pleased with her progress. Day 5 to 7 is critical for post-op infection. So there is a specific for prayer for the next 3 or 4 days.
—Prayer and blessings have gotten us this far. Thank you for all the support—near and far. I know she is feeling better because this morning she gave me "instructions" for plants in her yard and planters.
In thanksgiving for you . .

Mother Merdian

March 30, 2007—1:09pm

Who knew walking and sitting up could be such an exhausting task? Who didn't guess that hospital cream of wheat would leave a little something to be desired? Let's not even get into the gowns (more of a table cloth) and the sponge bath. Slowly, slowly, but mostly forward. Thanks for all the messages. I love reading them, and depending on medication levels, some of them seem new over and over again.

Yours 'til the epidural's back,

Sarah

March 30, 2007—9:22pm

Check out the new picture in the photo gallery...Antonio Banderas himself. He was anxious to share his thoughts about his new girlfriend, Sarah, and asked me to post a link to a short video clip where he tells all.

Mary

—⌇—

March 30, 2007—9:57pm

Yesterday, Dan and I flew down to Houston for a surprise visit for Sarah. (Yes, we cleared it thru Mother Merd first. Funny, that now Sarah doesn't want any more visitors....then again, Dan DID bring some lovely Gemmy products.) First, Dan tripped and almost tore out Sarah's epidural 'life line', but was forgiven after he showed her the interview with Antonio. (See the page photo gallery for a link to the video). Next, he played with the buttons on the hospital bed so that Sarah was upside down. Finally, he was asked to leave by the nurses when he plugged his computer speakers into the heart monitor which set off a loud beeping noise. Then Sarah showed us her stitches and Dan passed out.

Seriously, Sarah is incredibly brave—she had more stitches and staples than you could count, and it was amazing to see that she still had her sense of humor. She was making the nurses laugh and took every assault upon her dignity with grace and patience. Quite an inspiration to see. Watching her struggle to take a few very painful steps with the walker made me realize her unbelievable strength of will. She will need lots of love and support in the weeks ahead.

Mary

PS—Sarah requested no flowers or plants (really) because of her allergies. Cards are great-rm. G-1082

—⌇—

March 31, 2007—9:48pm
(You know the tune. I'm living it, so I figure you'd rather sing it.)

On the first day at MDA my doctors gave to me
A total hysterectomy

On the second day at MDA my doctors gave to me
Two leg pressure cuffs and
A total hysterectomy

On the third day at MDA my doctors gave to me
Three green mouth swabs
Two leg pressure cuffs and
A total hysterectomy

On the fourth day at MDA my doctors gave to me
Four cups of ice chips
Three green mouth swabs
Two leg pressure cuffs and
A total hysterectomy

On the fifth day at MDA my doctors gave to me
Five I.V. lines
Four cups of ice chips
Three green mouth swabs
Two leg pressure cuffs and
A total hysterectomy

And let's skip down to twelve

Twelve hours of surgery
Eleven sponges bathing
Ten Gemmy products

Nine is your pain
Eight drains a' draining
Seven insulin shots
Six beds a changing
Five I.V. lines
Four cups of ice chips
Three green mouth swabs
Two leg pressure cuffs and
A total hysterectomy

Yours 'til the Christmas carols,

Sarah

⌒⌒

April 02, 2007—11:11am

Short and sweet....just like many of my nurses. I am going home to my cousins' house today. I'm so happy to the idea of a really restful sleep (not quite that Rest in Peace eternal sleep, but close)

Thanks for all the positivity.

Yours 'til staple pulls,

Sarah

⌒⌒

April 03, 2007—05:50pm

Calling all helpers: If you are interested in helping Sarah when she returns to Dallas, please email either Teresa Khirallah (tkhirallah@yahoo.com) or myself (hansellm@esdallas.org) and we will send you an email with instructions on how to sign into the "Helping Hands" website. We are going to coordinate visits, meals, etc. using a centralized calendar on the Helping Hands website. You will be able to sign up for a specific date or time and Sarah will be able to let everyone know what she needs. A friend recommended it to Sarah and she thought it would be a good way to stay organized.

Any questions, please feel free to email me.

Thanks, Mary

April 05, 2007—10:14pm

THE TORTUGA TIMES (Weapons and mask not included in price of surgery)

Well, it seems that my body is now shaped like the old school Teenage Mutant Ninja Turtles. They were named for wonderful artists, right? And turtle speed sounds just about how my progress feels, but my class (especially Tres) will remind you how the turtle did in that famous race, so with many reminders....I'm hanging in there.

Yours 'til there's no hide of the hare,

Sarah

April 08, 2007—2:27pm

Sarah is at the E.R. at M.D. Anderson....she developed hives last night on her arms, and it spread to her legs and abdomen. Her leg swelled up this morning and they took her to the E.R. They think it might be an allergic reaction to the antibiotics she is taking, but the doctors are waiting for the results of the blood work to determine the cause. Sarah cannot have food or pain medication until they know the results. Please keep her in your prayers.

Mary

April 08, 2007—9:10pm

Sarah is back at her cousin's. The allergic reaction was from one of the antibiotics.

Thanks Mary, ...and I have to add that this morning when we heard from the on call doctor that I should go to the E.R., it was more than a little unnerving. We gathered things quickly, and locked up since my cousins had already headed out for Easter Mass.

Imagine our surprise to discover that we have picked up the WRONG car keys and locked the door on our way out of the house. My mother and sister proceed to run to the back door (also locked) as I stand in the driveway wearing a gown, robe, and shoes and holding my eight drains. It's about 45 degrees Fahrenheit and about 100% Keystone Cops. Well, my mother finally shouts out the location of the secret key (did all the neighbors hear that?) and they get back into the house and find the right set of keys for the car. The fun never stops, and neither do we.

I'm happy to be a little less itchy and scratchy. I go see both Dr. Butler and Dr. Coleman tomorrow. I'll keep you posted.

Yours 'til slap sticks,

Sarah

- ~

April 09, 2007—8:44pm

Heading back to Dallas! Today I met with Dr. Nigriny in Plastics and Dr. Coleman in Gyn Onc. Both cleared me to head back to Dallas and I'll return in two weeks for follow-up.

- Dr. Nigriny, who works with Dr. Butler, removed 3 of my 8 drains, but left all 200+ staples. He's taking me off pain meds and suggesting Advil. (Send truckloads at will, btw)
- Dr. Coleman is still uncertain about my pathology. It seems that the MD Anderson pathologists are somewhat divided on my "histology" (I think that means the slide specimens), and Dr. Coleman is consulting with an outside lab.
- There is no question about uterine cancer. The uncertainty concerns what type of cells were present

in the ovarian mass cysts. My abnormal abdominal cavity seems to add further confusion.

- Dr. Coleman still plans on chemo, but that won't start until I'm healed from my surgery. We'll know more in two weeks. I still got a hug and a kiss from Dr. Coleman. He's such a great guy.
- My sister thinks it would be neat if a new kind of cancer cell could be named after me. (Smerdinoma?) I'd be happy with an old familiar sort that already has an established chemo protocol.

I'm SO thankful for the hospitality of David and Loretta as well as for my mother's TLC. I know I am in such good shape because of all the wonderful care.

Monica and I head home on Gemmy Air tomorrow, and I'm looking forward to my own bed. The hives are getting better, and although I am exhausted today, I know I'm improving bit by bit. Thanks to Mary and TK for setting up the helping hands site. Thanks to everyone for their thoughts and support.

Yours 'til the pilot lights,

Sarah

April 12, 2007—8:34am

> *There's no place like home*
> **—overheard somewhere in Oz**

Well, thanks to the good folks at Air Flare, we made it home safely from the beautiful La Porte Municipal Airport. Mae West was not there to warn us of a bumpy ride, but Charles did mention that my sister Monica's face did almost match her green shirt. Happy to touch down.

I was greeted with a porch full of blossoms and even my roses are blooming outside my bedroom window. I'm starting to sleep a little better, and feel a little stronger every day. I've had one or two visitors. I wish I was up to seeing everyone. Patience, I'm told.

One thing I wanted to share was that during my hospital stay, I received 4+ units of blood. (Somehow, it seems very fitting that a teacher's blood type is A+.) If you are in a position to donate blood, I urge you to do it. Better yet, take a friend and share a pint that way.

Yours 'til the blood types,

Sarah

⌒〜〜

April 16, 2007—9:17am

"You mean it hasn't started already?" gasped Charles. Okay, so we all know that this is the best response to the statement, *"I'm worried about how I will be when the menopause starts."* Yes, welcome to the emotional rollercoaster. Luckily, there are always more ups than downs.

Here are a few highlights.

I'm happy to be able to sleep on my side. Of course, it requires a 6 point procedure involving the drain placement, pillows (both gushy and firm), and a careful "rolling", but it's great.

I'm handling most days with Advil rather than prescription pain meds.

I'm gaining ground most days in regards to being up and a little more active. Fatigue is certainly an issue.

I was welcomed home with a wonderful low-allergen bouquet and a great signed picture from my class. (I love hearing from my class. You go rock (as in sedimentary) on that science test this week.)

I'm getting FABULOUS dinners delivered to my house. The nutritionist suggested that I do 5 or 6 smaller meals each day, so having great stuff on hand is a blessing.

My sister stayed with me last week and Laura Daly is coming in today. I appreciate their patience.

The Flahertys sent over a power recliner (complete with 3 massage settings). I'm a little leery about using the power assist to get out of the chair because I'm afraid that Dan might have had a catapult setting added to the menu.

Mainly, I'm working on maintaining a positive mindset. Even though the drains are a pain, I appreciate that they are keeping me from developing infection in my incisions. I've come a long way from a breathing ventilator and ice chips and I'm thankful to be back home. Your continued support is appreciated. I head back to Houston for appointments on the 26th, so I plan to use this time to get stronger and stronger.

Yours 'til the rollercoaster rides,

Sarah

April 18, 2007—8:58am

> *She said she usually cried at least once each day*
> *not because she was sad, but because the world*
> *was so beautiful and a life was so short.*
> **—Brian Andreas, *Bittersweet***

Brian Andreas is an unusual artist and one of my favorites. (My sister hates his stuff). His work story people includes prints and abstract sculptures. I fell in love with his strange shapes, colors, lines, and right-on-the-money stories many years ago in Taos, and I bump into his work in the most unexpected places.

The weekend before my surgery, Mother, Charles, and I happened into a funky art shop on the Strand in Galveston. I was having a hard time keeping my mind from worrying about what "was to be", and then I discovered that the place is filled with Brian Andreas pieces. I can't really explain the comfort, calm, and peace that I felt surrounded by his work. I looked at every single print—probably over 50 and cried and laughed and felt strangely at home.

So now that I'm home and have discovered Brian Andreas' Storypeople website, I have decided to buy the Bittersweet sculpture. (It costs just a little more than a EKG and urine specimen, but will be enjoyed much more!) And thanks to Charles who knew just the right thing to say when I mentioned that I didn't know where I'd put it, and should that keep me from buying it. And so, I guess what I'm saying is

The world is beautiful and even the longest life is so short and shouldn't we always try to surround ourselves with that which we love?

Thanks for surrounding me. Yours 'til the bitter is sweet,

Sarah

—⁓—

April 18, 2007—7:49pm

If you are interested in helping Sarah with meals or rides, please email either Teresa Khirallah (tkhirallah@yahoo.com) or myself (hansellm@esdallas.org) and we will send you an email with instructions on how to sign into the "Helping Hands" website. We are going to coordinate visits, meals, etc. using a centralized calendar on the Helping Hands website. You will be able to sign up for a specific date or time and Sarah will be able to let everyone know what she needs. Any questions, please feel free to email me.

Thanks, Mary Hansell

—⁓—

April 20, 2007—11:47pm

> *Breath is the bridge which connects life to consciousness,*
> *which unites your body to your thoughts.*
> **Thich Nhat Hanh**

For many years in 5th grade, the remedy to most minor ills has been the wet paper towel. It holds acknowledgement, distraction, action, comfort, and possibility. That's quite a talent for wet paper, yet I'm learning that a breath can do so much more.

It seems simple enough, but someone had to remind me. Thanks to DK for working with breathing and meditation with me last fall as a way to handle all the thoughts racing around my head.

The physical therapists wanted me to exhale as I stood up with the walker. The IV Team urged calm breathing (top score-six sticks before we got a line.), and the respiratory team was all over breathing and coughing and clearing out my lungs. In this past month, deliberate, focused breathing has gotten me through pain, fear, sadness, despair, a feeling of losing control, impatience, frustration, and time.

> Breathe in
> Breathe out
> Relax
> Enjoy
> Endure
> Escape
> Emerge
> Have a great weekend.

Yours 'til the breath mints,

Sarah

—◦—

April 23, 2007—11:11pm

> *There is not a truth existing which I fear or would wish unknown to the whole world.*
> **Thomas Jefferson**

On Thursday, I'll see Dr. Coleman and hear what they've discovered, or decided, about my cancer. Unlike any other doctor's visit in my entire life, I go to this one with absolutely no fear whatsoever.

I've always been at least somewhat afraid about what a doctor, or evaluator, or therapist, or a test might tell me, and more than once, I've avoided pursuing the truth because the fear was just too great. Well, I couldn't feel more safe than I do right now. Anything that comes my way is what it is, and nothing more. I feel like I'm exactly where I'm supposed to be in this journey, and I will undertake whatever comes up next.

I don't know why we have such a difficult time believing that who we are today....right now...is okay, and worthy, and enough. Now, I'm not saying that I'm excited about chemo, menopause, and possibly radiation, but I'm not afraid. Whatever happens, it will be all right. I am and will be all right.

I know I haven't gotten to this place alone. The thoughts and prayers that have surrounded me throughout this whole ordeal have helped me arrive at this safe and calm place. I am beyond grateful. I'll keep you posted on what we find out.

Yours 'til there's no fearing fear itself,

Sarah

April 26, 2007—6:37pm

One step forward. One step sideways. I just got back from MDA and got to see my two boys (Drs. Butler and Coleman).

Dr. Butler (who told me that there was a 100% chance of infection in this procedure but told my mother that there was a 200% chance) is very happy with my progress. In fact, he's somewhat amazed. And of course, I got to go through another round of pictures against the blue wall.

I was more than slightly disappointed that they only removed one drain. (That leaves two. Their names are now Doctor and

Butler). I've had sort of a love/hate relationship with the drains. I hate having them and I love that they do such good work for me. They are preventing infection. Doctor and Butler will stay in until their output dwindles. They will most likely be removed in Dallas. They removed about half of my staples. They left the center section—the fleur de lis—intact. I'm supposed to go back to see them in 3 weeks.

Dr. Coleman wants me to start chemo in the next two weeks. I will have 6 rounds of chemo. Each will be "a long day" and the sessions will be three weeks apart. Luckily, I can do chemo in Dallas. I'll meet with Dr. Koon at Baylor, probably next week. (Dr. Coleman is excited for Dr. Koon to see the results of my surgery. "*He'll be amazed.*") No further word on the pathology yet, however the results will not affect the chemotherapy treatment decisions.

I did ask if my daily emotional upsets (the rollercoaster) were the result of:

    A. Major surgery
    B. You've got cancer
    C. My life doesn't feel like my life
    D. Menopause

and the answer was probably all of the above. Neat.

If anyone knows the Dance of the Dwindling Drain (please, try to say that three times quickly), send over the instructions.

Yours 'til the baby steps,

                              Sarah

April 30, 2007—6:44pm

If one of my students loses a tooth, I remind them that legend has it that a pure gold tooth will grow if you DON'T put your tongue in the hole left by the old one.

Well, I'm sort of experiencing the same difficulty. On the top half of my vertical incision, right where the staples were removed last week, I've found two little pieces of what appears to be fishing line, sticking right out of the scar. Now if I pull on them.....just ever so slightly....they'll come out of my body about 1/4 inch and go back in when released. Joe Flaherty chided me and told me to stop or I might "unravel completely."

Here's my question: Does that mean the phrase will no longer be a metaphor for how this whole experience affects a person?

Yours 'til the self controls,

Sarah

PS—I can drive

PSS—My Bittersweet story person arrived today. Yippee!

May 04, 2007—9:38am

> *As your faith is strengthened you will find that there is no longer the need to have a sense of control, that things will flow as they will, and that you will flow with them, to your great delight and benefit.*   **Emmanuel Teney**

The last month of school has always been a joy to me.....not because we're almost finished.....but because it was a time for me to step back and let my students spread their wings. Without fail, they always show me their independence, their confidence, the application of all they've learned, their ability to take risks, work as a team, assume responsibility, and think.

I'm always there to be their "guide on the side," but I must say that seeing them not need me in order to be successful is one of my greatest joys as a teacher. I feel like I'm missing out this year. Perhaps they got the chance earlier.

It's certainly not easy for me to relinquish control, but I guess being able to do this means that I have faith in what I have taught them and that I have faith in their ability to make wise choices on their own. Parents who have graduating seniors must feel the same way.

I have felt confident that I've been at the right place along this journey even though every step has had its own difficulties. Next Monday I go see Dr. Koon to set up my chemo schedule. I'm hoping that I can let go of my need for control and continue to have faith that this will all work out the way it's supposed to be. Have a great weekend.

Yours 'til May flies,

Sarah

May 07, 2007—2:46pm

Well, just like a recurring nightmare, Girafferella, the abnormally long-necked wig mannequin, was staring down at me as I walked through the Baylor Sammons Cancer Center this morning. I tried not to make eye contact.

Dr. Koon had just spoken to Dr. Coleman and was quite impressed by my incision. I'm so thankful that they have a great working relationship and that I can benefit from both of them. I was not quite prepared to hear Dr. Koon tell me that I am considered a Stage IV MMMT because the cancer has spread into my abdominal cavity. Still no exact word on the other pathology, but it appears that it won't make a difference in treatment protocols.

It probably wasn't a good idea for me to Google STAGE IV MMMT because I found a couple of sites that said the 5 year survival rate for that stage is only about 10%. Now, I've taught Math long enough to know better, but I'm thinking if I beat Dr. Butler's 200%

chance of infection odds, then somehow there must be a way to work the two percentages together and have it come out in my favor. Seriously, I know that my body doesn't know anything about statistics and I can only hope for the strength to handle what is to be. I'm not looking forward to chemotherapy, but I am grateful for the opportunity it may provide.

Will attend a chemo class tomorrow, get a baseline CT scan and chest x-ray this week, and then I will start my chemotherapy next Tuesday, May 15th. I'll be receiving two cancer drugs: Taxol and Carboplatin, and then some other meds such as anti-nausea, etc. The chemo sessions will be about 5 or 6 hours long, and I'll have six sessions with three week intervals. I will go back to Dr. Koon during each interval for blood tests and assessment.

Hair loss is expected, so that tattoo wasn't inked in vain, and Beth, Dr. Koon's great nurse, gave me some resources for wigs although she said summer chemo patients usually prefer scarves and hats to wigs because of the heat. Charles has offered to shave my head and serve on the wig procurement team.

I guess recovering from surgery was round one (it's six weeks today), and here comes round two. I'm not down for the count yet.

Yours 'til all the world's a stage,

Sarah

———

May 09, 2007—7:42am

BY THE NUMBERS Earlier this week, the whole stage IV assessment was quite upsetting (but I'm fine now. A label is a label is a label) Here are some much more interesting numbers.

Total length of my incision: 48 inches
Number of staples left: 87
Post hospital amount of fluid removed by my 8 drains:
9399 ml

Total drains left: 0

Amount of EZ EM banana smoothie barium that I had to drink at 8 am and keep down before my ct scan: 450 ml

Number of bottles of a vineyard's finest that our foursome shared the night before: 3 (ouch)

Last night's temperature (I check every day for signs of infection): 97.7°

Pairs of dangle earrings that I have received: 27

Longest stretch of time without any tears: 3 days

Number of times per day that I am supposed to gargle with a baking soda, and salt water mixture to prevent mouth sores during chemo: 4 or more

Length of my typical chemo day: 7 to 8 hours

Complete dvd seasons of Arrested Development that I plan to watch during chemo (I need to take a break from the intensity of 24 and focus on laughing): 3

Number of Advil taken yesterday: 2

Number of Back Care mailings I've received from Life Masters: 3

Number of cancer mailings from Life Masters: 0

Number of diet cokes I've had since surgery: 0.5

Percent of days that I find something to laugh about: 100%

As of 7:15 this morning, the number of hits at the CarePage: 10,158 (wow that saved a lot of my rollover minutes! Thanks again Mim.)

Number of those hits that are from me reading and rereading your wonderful comments: 505

Yours 'til everything counts,

Sarah

May 11, 2007—11:11am

> *The thought of her teacher coming back.*
> *Yes, no she has no clue,*
> *The doubts of her never coming back,*
> *But keeping a positive attitude.*
> *Her teacher, a big help in life, who taught her so much.*
> *Now gone, but not forever.*
>
> **From "There was a Child went
> Forth" by Yesenia**

I visited school today. It was so great to see my 5th grade class. They have made a beautiful quilt for me. Some look taller and older, and my heart just ached that I've missed so much with them. Katy shared their poems based on Walt Whitman's "There was a Child went Forth."They would not have had that experience without her. Golden moments.

This week before chemo is coming to a close. I've taken care of some business and even got a wig from the American Cancer Society. It matches my hair although Charles did force me to try on a couple that were scary. Let's say I never need to look like a member of the 80s band THE ROMANTICS (That's what I like about you!) Dr. Butler's office informed me that I could have my remaining staples removed in Dallas, and I'll have that done after chemo on Tuesday.

This whole experience reminds me that there are two sides to every coin…..the up and down……the yin and yang,

- Clarity of spirit and sense of loss.
- Feeling both a sense of connection and distance after my visit to school.

- Dreading and welcoming chemotherapy.
- Gratitude for all of the support surrounding me and frustration at not being my independent self.

Cancer doesn't create these dichotomies, but perhaps it is letting me accept, appreciate and understand them a little better.

Yours 'til the fifth goes forth,

Sarah

PS—Have a great weekend and Happy Mother's Day!

May 15, 2007—5:11pm

> *It's always something.* —Gilda Radner

Well, one chemo session down, and five to go. Today was okay. I napped through some of the session; it ended up being about six hours total. Right now I have a dull headache, some aches, and a sore hand. I did get all of my staples removed afterwards and I am THRILLED.

I have heard SO MUCH about possible side effects, and I'm really curious (nervous?) to see which ones will affect me. Today's nurse said that she didn't think I'd have much nausea at all, but I do have preventative meds. She also told me that on day three I would get joint and muscle pain and feel like I have the flu. Everybody is a little different I guess. The only constant it seems is hair loss. I go cueball next week. I'll be sure to post a picture.

I did have an unexpected delight this weekend. I attended a new member meeting at Gilda's Club here in Dallas. I couldn't be more impressed with the organization. It's founded in honor of Gilda Radner of SNL fame who died of ovarian cancer in 1989. They offer social and emotional support for cancer patients, families, and friends. They have support groups (I'll start mine next Monday evening), social activities such as book clubs, art classes, game nights and potluck dinners, and educational programs on nutrition, meditation, exercise, etc. The rooms are wonderfully furnished and comfortable and who wouldn't love to meet in the Roseanne Roseannadanna or Emily Litella (violins on TV) room? It's all good.

Now that the staples are out, the only other thing I'm working on is RESISTING the temptation to go into a piercing place, pay for a belly button ring, and then watch the tech try to find it.

Thanks for all of the support sent my way. Today was a tough day to face, and even though I chose to go by myself, I never felt alone.

Yours 'til love's in vein,

Sarah

May 16, 2007—10:45pm

The Fast Track

Well, my nurse told me to expect Benadryl grogginess on day one, steroid induced "crawling out of my skin" on day two, and flu-like aches and pains on days three to five.

I feel like I'm in the advanced class because the grogginess left just when I tried to sleep last night. I got the creepy crawlies at midnight, and this afternoon the muscle and joint aches just knocked me down and here come those tears again.

Now, the good news is that I did feel great this morning and made it to Target and then to Weir's for a new coffee table. Shopping therapy.

The best news so far is that the anti-nausea medications seem to be working. I felt quite queasy this afternoon, but so far, so good. Here we go day three.

Yours 'til I'm not Chemo-sobby,

Sarah

May 18, 2007—10:30am

Yesterday I got cleared to start swimming again, and since a pool is just a big ol' bathtub, I figured that I'd test the waters (so to speak) by taking a bath. My chemo aches were certainly soothed by the relaxing warmth. However, I seemed to have forgotten how hard it is for me to even get out of certain chairs in my house.........hmm, how about getting out of a bathtub? I have decided that I am my own heavy machinery that the prescription bottles warn against operating.

Yet, with prayers of thanks to both the good Lord and Archimedes......in conjunction with grunts, moans, and some abdominal distress.......I did make it out on my own.

My side effects are calming down a bit. I'm sleeping better, the aches are not quite as severe, and I am getting a little bit of an appetite. Post-op mouth sores have gotten much worse, and I'm getting a prescription mouthwash from Baylor today. I spoke to the nurse this morning and she suggests that I keep taking the anti-nausea medication since I still feel queasy (but still no vomiting Did I ever think I'd be sharing that as my good news of the day?)

Here's to keeping spirits up and lunch down.

Yours 'til the bathtub rings,

Sarah

——◆——

May 21, 2007—12:12pm

Nothing says confidence-builder like having the 90-year-old "just got my hip replacement" woman walk faster in the therapy pool than you can swim. Well, that and hearing her tell her friend, "Well, maybe he'll try to kiss me on our second date." The good thing about the pool is that no one can tell you're crying.

Actually, this was my second visit to the fitness center, and I managed to swim or walk for 20 minutes. I keep reading that exercise will help with the chemo fatigue. Turns out you need more than just the heart of athlete, I guess.

Tonight I attend my first support group at Gilda's Club, and it looks like Wednesday will be the big balding. Hopefully Charles can be talked out of the experimental styles he wants to fashion in the process. (Just say NO to flattops and Mohawks.)

Yours 'til the buzz cuts,

Sarah

———

May 24, 2007—7:49am

Well, thanks to Charles, I now am a member of the Cancer Bald Head Club. It's not nearly as bad as I thought it would be. (Although the part when he vacuumed off half my face was quite surprising.) Charles had such a fun time.

As for the rest of the week, I found out that my current blood work all looks good. I had a great time at school during carpool yesterday, I got a wonderful post-chemo massage at Baylor, and sorry, but the $400 cell phone bill means fewer calls before 9 pm and weekends. (I'm looking in to this being a tax-deduction medical expense and yes, I've changed my plan....sorta) I feel much stronger than I did a week ago.

Yours 'til the hat tricks,

Sarah

———

May 27, 2007—8:25pm

> ***You look like a man with earrings.***
> **—Kindergarten observation**

Actually, they were great and inquisitive. They were interested in cancer but when their teacher asked if the tattoo hurt, then the kids were really intrigued. I can only describe the group cringe that followed the mentioning of a needle as a version of synchronized swimming or the choreography of those little Meer cats. I enjoyed my time up at school this week, and I probably feel better than I have in months.

One thing I want to mention is how appreciative I am for all of the love, support, cards, food, and favors that have been showered upon me. I can't remember who has received a thank you note or e-card, but I do know that I've been horribly remiss about expressing my gratitude.

After my broken ankle, I had a THANKLE party to celebrate and thank everyone for their help during that awful time. I don't quite know how the words endometrial, tumor, chemo or cancer will fit cleverly into a party theme invitation, but I've got a few months to work on it. I'll keep you posted. Until then, please know that I am beyond grateful to all of you.

Yours 'til the party favors,

Sarah

May 31, 2007—8:34am
Conversation in the blood lab waiting room at Baylor:

Complete Stranger—Is your tattoo a Tibetan symbol?
Sarah—No, it's a personal design created by a friend.
CS—Well, it's great. This is my second time with cancer. I don't think I'm brave enough like you to just go bald, but I hate the wigs and the scarves and the hats. I don't know.
SM—So far, so good, but it's just been a week and it hasn't been sunny.
CS—I'm sure I'll see you around. YOU'RE PRETTY HARD TO MISS.
SM.....just smiles and nods.

The good news is that my blood work all looks good. My sleep number bed arrived, I had a dinner party last night, and I'm taking a short trip to KC this weekend before I hit chemo next week. I sort of overdid it yesterday, but I did get to laugh a LOT.

Hope everyone has a great weekend. It might even stop raining.

Yours 'til this Miss is missed,

Sarah

⌐ ⌐

June 04, 2007—9:26am

> *If it weren't for my mood swings, I wouldn't get any exercise at all.*
>
> **—gift magnet from a KC friend**

Actually, I also get quite the workout from jumping to conclusions and jogging my memory, but we'll save my fun with "chemo brain" for another day,

I had a grand time in Kansas City. Seeing so many wonderful friends is good for my soul. Now, if only my body can catch up. Despite the "exercise will combat fatigue" assertion, I find myself drained each and every day. I apologize to everyone that I didn't get to see or call. I was able to catch up on a little bit of sleep since my return flight was diverted to Wichita Falls due to storms in Dallas.

It's certainly lovely to be the center of attention, but there are always those grounding (and humbling) moments like when a 3 year old inspects your bald head and then insists that you go ahead and put the hat back on. (Daddy, MY hair doesn't fall out when I take medicine…..)

I can't say that I'm looking forward to my second round of chemo on Wednesday. I guess it's sort of like the dread I feel going to Home Depot. Not only is the time spent there painful, but then you've got to do the rest of the project when you get home. Thank goodness the chemo nurses don't wear orange aprons.

I'm scheduled to go to the American Cancer Society's "Look Good Feel Better" class today. I think it's all about make-up tips and how to do origami head scarves or something. Oy vey. Perhaps I'd feel more comfortable in the "If Looks Could Kill" class.

Yours 'til the eye shadows,

Sarah

———

June 07, 2007—2:04pm

Why was I thinking that my second chemo day would be any less fun that my first one? Here are some highlights:

- Dr. Koon's first questions were......... *"Has it really been a month since I've seen you? How was chemo?"* Well, it's always nice to be missed, and yes, just a month since a very comprehensive cavity search (no one mentioned this would occur at EVERY visit), and to be honest, chemo's not that much fun. He did give me some meds for the body aches, and he did make all the correct comments on my tattoo.
- My chemo nurse reminded me of Debbie Downer from SNL. After her first needle stick didn't find a vein, she told me that she was having a bad day and got another nurse. (It took three needle sticks to start the iv line. Ouch! I couldn't help crying. Always a good start. Who's having the bad day?)
- I did get the room with the bed rather than the recliner in the open market style stall. That was great.
- The new blood pressure cuff was CRUSHING my arm, so I mentioned that last time they took the

reading on my forearm. After the nurse took 4 consecutive readings in 3 minutes, my high diastolic number puzzled her. She asked, "Are you under any kind of stress?" My response, "Well, I am in CHEMOTHERAPY."

- The drip went faster this time, and Charles dropped me off at home a little after 4:00. Imagine my surprise to walk in and discover that yes, on the warmest day so far this season, my power was completely out. Nice to be in the sauna.

- I have received 4 phone books in the last week, and I could not find a listing for the electric company. (One of the new phonebooks is in Spanish, but still no luck) Thanks to Ann Casey for being so close to the top of my cell phone list; she kindly found a customer service number online. A transformer was out and they expected it to be repaired by 7 pm. (actual time—9:06 pm)

- The Hansells made a surprise visit and Elise was sweet enough to fan me with my brand new Cancer Survivors Week Fan. Unfortunately, her rapid air current sent some sort of dust particle into my eye. Well, it didn't swell completely shut.

DOES THE FUN EVER START? Yet somehow, it just all makes me laugh.

I felt pretty good yesterday evening, and then the creepy crawling-out-of-my-skin set in a little after midnight. Not really a good night's sleep, but I popped my first anti-nausea pill this morning and I swear that's what kept breakfast down as I was planting flowers and a slug fell off the flower pot and rolled down my entire leg. It's nice get the full benefit of your medication. I'm starting to feel a little achy and I think it's time for a pain pill and a nap. I hope to be on the mend by the weekend.

Yours 'til the breaker boxes,

Sarah

PS—I LOVE my mosaic mirror. KC friends painted tiles and created quite the masterpiece. I'm sure Charles will tell me where it goes.

June 09, 2007—2:27pm

Calling all able-bodied locals!! This Tuesday, June 12th, I will be packing up my classroom, and I would appreciate any and all help. I still can't lift much, but I can point and sort. We'll be starting at 9 am at Peak Academy (4605 Live Oak, Dallas, TX 75204), but feel free to come (or go) at any time. The entrance gate is on Bryan Street.

If you're willing and available, let me know. My home email is smerd@excite.com and cell phone is 214.460.6466. All—and I mean all—are welcome. Bring a drink and I'll provide pizza for lunch! Thanks so much,

Yours 'til the cardboard boxes,

Sarah

PS—Hoped to be finished with the chemo effects by today, but s omehow my body wasn't notified. Fingers crossed for tomorrow.

June 14, 2007—3:15pm

Today as I was walking to the pool through the locker room, an older lady just came up and gave me a big hug. *"You're in chemo, right? Bless you."* It was so touching. I hadn't been up to swimming for over a week, so it felt good AND completely draining. I'm happy to have graduated to the big pool, and I can even use the ladder to get out (with minimal groaning.)

I really didn't expect the effects of my second chemo to be more long-lasting than the first. It took a week to feel better, or to get back to what my support group folks refer to my "new normal." It's a good way to look at this (although you'd think I'd have the "it's all about me" part down pat by now!)

Thanks to the many helping hands that packed up my classroom this week. We topped out at 125 boxes, and Charles was quite adroit at redirecting my focus when I started to get melancholy about moving out of the classroom.

I must mention my "Look Good, Feel Better" class. I didn't expect it to be so great. (I hear it used to be called "Look Good, Feel Good", but someone realized that feeling "better" might be a more realistic hope). The scarf and wig portion weren't really my thing, but the make-up tips were great, and I'm sure both Charles and my sister are thinking, *"Finally, she gets it; she's a girl."*

Thanks to the many cosmetic companies (Mary Kay, Clinique, Revlon, Chanel, Avon, Estee Lauder, etc.) who donated supplies. We each got a goodie bag with over $150 worth of quality cosmetics. Everyone got the same basic items but they were all different vendors.

One hot item was a cool Estee Lauder compact that had a jeweled zodiac sign on the top. I got Sagittarius and another couple of gals had Gemini. We asked if these were anyone's signs just in case they'd like to trade. The big laugh of the session came when one lady asked, "Does anyone have Cancer?" Nice to see a dozen bald headed women laughing and raising their hands. (Who ever decided that Cancer should be a disease AND a zodiac sign anyway? No one ever gets a diagnosis of pancreatic Pisces or colon Capricorn. Really. And yes, born on July 21st, I am a Cancer).

Happy Father's Day to everyone. Have a great week.

Yours 'til the zodiac signs,

Sarah

Which of the following phrases did Dr. Coleman use to describe my pathology reports?

  A. Unique phenomenon
  B. So cool
  C. Very rare
  D. Good for all of us

Yes, of course the answer is ALL OF THE ABOVE.

I finally heard from Dr. Coleman regarding the path findings. He was so apologetic about not getting back in touch with me. *"Are you sure we haven't talked about this? I've been talking about it to everyone. I just did a presentation at a joint conference. I'm so sorry I forgot to talk to you."*

After my surgery, Dr. Coleman wanted further testing on my specimens since the MDA pathologists could not come to a consensus on their findings. They were trying to find out if the ovarian tumors were the result of the spreading of my uterine tumor. After further molecular mutation profiles at an outside facility, they have discovered that I actually have TWO types of cancer, uterine and ovarian, which have developed independently.

I asked how this would affect me besides the need to change my cancer ribbon color, and Dr. Coleman replied, *"Now you get to wear BOTH!"* Purple and peach one of each!

They were able to determine that the ovarian cancer started in my right ovary, spread to the left, and then to lymph nodes. It appears that the MMMT in my uterus had not spread. This seems to be good news because the MMMT is aggressive and, as Dr. Koon put it, "a heavy hitter." It looks like the uterine cancer has been removed at surgery and the ovarian cancer is being attacked with chemo. I feel hopeful.

The ovarian cancer aspect does not change my current course of treatment, but the new diagnosis could affect further treatment, perhaps even participation in clinical trials. I will return to MDA after my last chemo treatment.

Dr. Coleman also commented that this case is showing the MDA folks that they need to increase their technology so they can analyze specimens at this level. My case is *helping all of us down here.* I can't express the excitement I heard in Dr. Coleman's voice. Just when I thought I couldn't feel more special.

Yours 'til twice is nice,

Sarah

———— ◦————

June 20, 2007—5:10pm

- Periwinkle
- Yew tree
- Mayapple
- Asian "Happy Tree"

I know this looks like a shopping list for the local nursery, but actually, these plants are the sources for my chemotherapy drug called Taxol. I cannot even begin to fathom the research and development process that led up to this life-saving medication. Dr. Coleman was unwilling to accept inconclusive results and sought application of recently developed technology unavailable at M.D. Anderson.

Cancer treatment and technology have advanced by leaps and bounds in the past decade, past year, and who knows what breakthroughs happened today or might happen tomorrow.

This week I found out that a donation was made in my name to the American Cancer Society, and my sister asked me what I wanted for my birthday next month.

I have everything that I need.

I have a wonderful supportive community comprised
of friends, students, healthcare providers and family,
I have choices,
I have opportunities.
I have laughter in my life every day.
I have cancer (two kinds!).
I have hope.

I would love a birthday donation made to any cancer research organization. A lady in my support group says, *"I'm working on staying alive long enough for them to figure out the cure."*

Here's to many more birthdays.

Yours 'til the gift keeps on giving,

Sarah

June 25, 2007—9:17pm

I felt sorry when I had no shoes until I met a man who had no feet.

I've been feeling a little down lately because my life these days seems to be filled with waiting until the arrival of the next thing doctor's appointment, chemo, feeling bad after chemo, feeling better after feeling bad, etc. rather than living in the present. The frequent fatigue and uncertainty of "how will I feel today" haven't made me really angry, but more like I'm almost grieving the loss of who I used to be.

One book suggested that patients often feel like their illness is consuming their lives, but suggested that we try to view the situation differently. We can choose to say that managing our illness is currently a full-time job. I try to stay positive, but I'm not always successful.

Well, going to my support group this evening left me feeling somewhat ashamed of my own self-absorption. The group included:

- A man whose cancer has spread to his lungs, liver, and spleen.
- A woman who has just discovered black mold in her apartment (perhaps why she was in the hospital for 12 days after her last chemo with double pneumonia) and will most likely need to move right before her surgery.
- A breast cancer survivor who was diagnosed two months after the birth of her twin sons.
- A woman who, after finishing 36 rounds of chemo, had to fight with her "former" doctor for 9 days to get antibiotics for a respiratory infection.

Additional members also shared their stories, and each and every single person there was able to share a vision of hope, support, and laughter. I was given the gift of perspective this evening.

This doesn't really change the fact that I am not looking forward to chemo on Wednesday, and that I am dreading the discomfort of the ensuing side effects. I think it's okay to be honest about my struggles, feelings, and doubts, but I have certainly been reminded of my countless blessings and opportunities. I need to....I want to.....always remain grateful for all I have and hopeful for what will come.

Yours 'til the mountain's a molehill,

Sarah

June 27, 2007—9:53pm
RIBBON ALERT (with apologies to poets everywhere)

Two cancers have I,
A ribbon for each
I was mistaken

With purple and peach
Ovarian cancer
Turns out to be TEAL
This ribbon awareness
Is quite an ordeal.

The awareness game
Is blowing my mind.
You can't imagine
Ribbon colors assigned.
I do not poke fun
At any condition
So proceed with caution
At your own volition.

Breast cancer is pink.
AIDS awareness is red.
Yellow supports troops
Wherever they head.
Green's quite a list.
Transplant surviving,
Literacy, Glaucoma
Darfur and Safe Driving

Orange is Agent Orange
(No rhyme, oh rats!)
Cultural Diversity,
And yes, FERAL CATS.
Light green's STDs
Brain Cancer is gray,
Dyslexia's silver (sliver?)
Cranberry's TMJ

White's for adoption,
Hernias; anti-porn views,
Postpartum depression,
(Wear one, Tom Cruise)
Of course black is mourning,
But in all fairness,
My favorite black ribbon
Is for AMISH AWARENESS

(Okay, I hate to break cadence, but how does an Amish person order a ribbon from an internet website? They can't need the car magnet.....can they even use a safety pin?)

Now color combos,
I dare not mention,
Two and three colors,
Distract my attention.
These ribbons mean comfort
To so many we know,
And why yes, today—
Free time in chemo.

Yours 'til color's my world,

Sarah

--- ~ ---

July 02, 2007—12:24am

What can't be cured must be endured.

Everytime I get a twinge or an ache, I just think.....*Take That, Cancer! I'm not doing anything to help you.*

If my cancer cannot be cured, then I'll do my best to endure. I think I might have been called stubborn before. I can do that again. I don't feel particularly strong during these chemo rounds, but I do feel committed and supported by everyone.

I hope I'm coming into the homestretch of Chemo Round 3. It's been an achy breaky weekend. Body joint, muscles, and even toe aches, rashes, fatigue, and everyone's friend: nausea.

Dr. Koon was on vacation, so I saw Dr. Matthews last week. She is a nature girl and suggested a couple things for me including a hot-as-you-can-stand-it and cold-as-you-can-stand-it shower ritual to help with the aches and pains. Well, mainly, it seemed to be simply the I'M BURNING and I'M FREEZING and whew won't I be glad when the shower is just over and I can just go back to body aches.

She also suggested an Anti Inflammatory Diet, which looks like good common sense. Lots of fruits and vegetables, limited processed foods, and varied protein sources. However, reading about salmon, nut butters, and soy products was not the best thing right around anti-nausea pill time. Chemo affects your smell and even concept of food. I'll look more at the menu later in the week.

So, it's three rounds down and three to go. The glass is both half empty and half full. On any given day, so are we all. Here's to keeping spirits up and doubts at bay.

Yours 'til the toe jams,

Sarah

July 04, 2007—12:41pm

FIREWORKS! is my favorite Schoolhouse Rock song (Sorry all you "I'm Just a Bill" diehards.) Here's to the pursuit of happiness!

> *Ooh, there's gonna be fireworks (Fireworks!)*
> *On the Fourth of July (red, white, and blue!)*

Red, white, and blue fireworks
Like diamonds in the sky. (diamonds in the sky!)
We're gonna shoot the entire works on fireworks
That really show, oh yeah,
We declared our liberty 200 years ago.
Yeah!

In 1776 (fireworks!)
There were fireworks too (red, white, and blue!)
The original colonists,
You know their tempers blew (They really blew!)
Like Thomas Paine once wrote:
It's only common sense (only common sense)
That if a government won't give you your basic rights
You'd better get another government.

And though some people tried to fight it,
Well, a committee was formed to write it:
Benjamin Franklin, Philip Livingston,
John Adams, Roger Sherman, Thomas Jefferson,
They got it done (Oh yes they did!)
The Declaration, uh—huh—huh,
The Declaration of Independence (Oh yeah!)
In seventeen hundred seventy six (Right on!)
The Continental Congress said that we were free (We're free!)
Said we had the right of life and liberty,
...And the pursuit of happiness!

Ooh, when England heard the news, (Kerpow!)
They blew their stack (They really blew their cool!)
But the colonies lit the fuse,
There'd be no turning back (no turnin' back!)

They'd had enough of injustice now
But even if it really hurts, oh yeah,
If you don't give us our freedom now
You're gonna see some fireworks!

And on the Fourth of July they signed it
And 56 names underlined it,
And now to honor those first 13 states,
We turn the sky into a birthday cake.
They got it done (Oh yes they did!)
The Declaration, uh huh huh,
The Declaration of Independence (Oh yeah!)
In seventeen hundred seventy six (Right on!)
The Continental Congress said that we were free (We're free!)
Said we had the right of life and liberty,
...And the pursuit of happiness!

We hold these truths to be self-evident,
That all men are created equal
And that they are endowed by their creator
With certain inalienable rights.
That among these are life, liberty, and the pursuit of
   happiness.

And if there's one thing that makes me happy,
Then you know that it's (ooh)
There's gonna be fireworks! [1]

Yours 'til the truth's self-evident,

Sarah

PS—A week out of chemo 3. More fatigue, more nausea, more
   fun! Mother will be joining me to help out for round 4.

  Sarah Merdian

Someone told me *"It's all downhill from here."* Hmm, it's pretty much all been downhill. I'm looking for the upswing.

~-~

July 05, 2007—10:47pm

A picture is worth a thousand words.

No one ever said that they would be a thousand NICE words. I'm always a little hesitant when I see the insurance company's name in the return address portion of an envelope. I've become quite familiar with the "Explanations of Benefits" mailings, but today's offering just looked different.

Imagine my surprise to receive a copy of a letter addressed "Dear PROVIDER" which requested "PRE-OPERATIVE PHOTOS". Right away I'm thinking….hmm….wonder if they'd like a copy of last year's Christmas card photo in front of the Taj Mahal.

The letter also asked for "Documentation of all treatments for INTERTRIGO from the surgeon." Now, of course I've never heard of intertrigo, but I'm betting that the only happy place to see it is on a scrabble board (triple word score).

Turns out intertrigo is the inflammation of skin around body folds. Ick. My insurance company is asking for photographic evidence of belly chafing? Isn't a double shot of cancer enough? No one told me that I got a bonus side order of intertrigo. (Although apparently the insurance company is having trouble with that additional service charge.)

I had pretty much (and this will be the only use of the word pretty in this posting) buried the "stand-bucky-nake-in-front-of-the-blue-wall" photo session in Dr. Butler's office. I'd almost forgotten the four other people in the room and the black and purple industrial sharpie marks all over my abdomen. Now I get to relive that fun moment AND imagine the insurance company employees "reviewing" my case.

Dr. Butler told me that my face wouldn't be in the photos. (I had offered to smile if he wanted.) Luckily, I have that unmistakable tattoo to provide clear identification.

Lord, please don't let this become this year's Christmas card.

I did call the insurance company to get some further info. They are reviewing Dr. Butler's billing claims. I mentioned that the man worked very hard on me and that I'd love to see him compensated for his efforts. The fun never stops!

Yours 'til the shutter flies,

Sarah

July 09, 2007—08:19am

I had a quiet weekend, but like others in Dallas, was thrilled to see the sun poke through on several occasions. We are tired of all of this rain.

A couple evenings of dinner and scrabble with friends (yes, aren't they shameless for playing with a chemo brain?) were filled with lots of laughs, but the big news is that I finally got my iPhone working. I can't blame Apple for my activation delay. I guess most techno geeks would already have the 2 yr. old operating system upgrade on their computers. I had to wait (impatiently) for mine to arrive FedEx.

Well, of course, I just love the phone. I plan on taking it instead of the laptop to chemo next time. Watching a couple episodes of The Office or just listening to the iPod will make the time go by more quickly. I'll check with the accountant, but this just might be a medical expense. Unfortunately/fortunately, iTunes makes it VERY EASY to download new songs and videos with the slightest click.

No real news. I am battling constant fatigue. My anemia seems to be a player in all of this. I hope to meet with Dr. Koon this week before chemo to discuss some options. At times, the fatigue is really debilitating. I know I make a great fruit salad, but I don't think I should have to lie down for a rest afterwards.....(well, there were peaches....)

This week's "cancer a-ha" moment, you know the one that you just don't see coming, was "where has all my nose hair gone?" I don't know why that realization surprised me, but it did. No one had mentioned it. Turns out both nose hair and eyelashes do quite a good job in the filter and protection areas. Friends have offered to lend me some (even from ears?!?!), but I'm struggling through.

Have a great week. Looks like I'm going to get to do some curriculum work for school this week. I'm looking forward to it.

Yours 'il hair today, gone tomorrow,

Sarah

~⚬~

July 12, 2007—8:55am

Cancer patients have blood work done weekly so the doctors can monitor our white and red blood cell levels (plus a list of other test results a page long that I don't really understand.) Baylor patients sign in, park it in the waiting area, and are called back in groups of 4 or 5 to the lab. We enter one room and take one of the many chairs lining the wall.

Barry has been my main phlebotomist since I've been there. He looks like he used to be a football player and he has the most gentle touch with the needle. Betty has another patient let's call her Hilda because she looks a lot like my grandmother and they are harping on Barry something fierce.

I guess Hilda has been trying to get Barry to sing for her. *"I've heard you have a good voice, but I don't have any real evidence. I'm a good singer, too. I want you to sing "Amazing Grace" because that's what they're playing when I die, and if you're good, I'm calling the funeral home and giving them your name. Now go, 1......2.......3."*

Well, Barry has been shaking his head no and saying "*I don't want to sing a song that will make you think you have to die right now.*" But when Hilda gets to the number 3, he stops (needle still in my arm), and the most angelic voice BOOMS out of him. You would expect to hear that verse of "Amazing Grace" from the soloist at the Gospel Church. Simply amazing. It even got an AMEN! from me.

Well, we all loved it, and then Betty turns to Hilda and says, "*Looks like it's GO TIME for you, Sister.*" Hilda's eyes get big, and Barry lets out a "*Oh no she didn't.*" and I gasp and laugh. Then Betty realizes that we think GO TIME means time to die, and she starts stammering about how it means time for Hilda to sing. We all laugh and Barry wraps the bandage on my arm, and it's been three minutes since I sat down in his chair.

On my way out, I see another patient—an elderly gentleman—lean over to his phlebotomist and say, "*Tell me if you've heard this one. Three vampires walk in to a blood bank.....*"

Cancer has brought me so many of these moments filled with a celebration of peace, laughter, and shared humanity between near strangers. Somehow our defensive outer layers have been stripped away, and what we've been taught to politely ignore is right there in our faces. One time, I sat down in Barry's chair almost crying and rather than ignore the tears, he wants to know how it's his lucky day. He's getting tears for free. He didn't even have to stick me to get tears. Maybe he should go buy a lottery ticket, and so forth. Of course, I ended up laughing and vying for a smart aleck comeback for him.

I can't say it's all good, but it's far from all bad.

Yours 'til it saves a wretch like me,

Sarah

July 17, 2007—8:19am

Yesterday I got a wonderful massage (Kathleen at Spa Nordstrom—love her), and I came home feeling relaxed and calm. I took a quick nap and somehow that massage must have opened the floodgates of emotion because I ended up a crying, sobbing, ranting mess.

I was supposed to go out to dinner with a few friends and somehow just couldn't bring myself to do it. All of these fears rushed to the surface....What if this is my last birthday? What if this pain in my abdomen is more cancer? What are these lymph-like bumps on my body? Why has my temperature gone up 0.5 degrees in the last two days? (just to 98.3)

I realize (then and now) that this was not rational thought, and I really do try to stay positive and keep those demons of doubt at bay. I remember thinking during my massage that I was releasing all my negativity and letting it go. I guess I just hadn't gotten all of the way out of my system yet.

Several people have mentioned that I seem so strong and seem to be handling all of this. Well, the secret's out. Not always. I felt anything but strong last evening, and sometimes that just happens. I don't see it coming, and thank God for Charles because I don't know how I could break out of that cycle on my own. (If you don't have a Charles, well, you can't have mine, but do get yourself one.)

I ended up having a delightful evening. Good food, good wine, great laughs, great company. I am blessed to have such wonderful friends who are willing to love me even when I'm a mess.

I have my fourth chemo this Thursday, and I'll see Dr. Koon and run my bumps and aches by him. My mother is coming into town to help me get through those side effects during the next week. I've been doing some curriculum work for school and I'm looking forward to a presentation on Wednesday. It will be nice to feel like I can contribute something.

Yours 'til I'm rubbed the right way,

Sarah

July 19, 2007—11:29pm

Today in the chemo infusion room, I asked my nurse if I could use one of the rooms with a hospital bed rather than the recliner. I had a horrible night's sleep last night and figured I could really use the rest. Her response was *"We usually try to save the beds for people who are sick. Are you sick?"* Okay, I'm thinking that just being in chemo counts as "being sick." Hello! I have two kinds of cancer. At least she went on to say that usually older people used it (I felt so young), and needless to say, I napped in the recliner today.

Chemo went okay, except I got those creepy crawlies at the very same time that I was super groggy from the Benadryl. It's strange to be bouncing with restless legs and squirming about when you can't manage to hold up your head or keep your eyelids open.

It seems like my side effect timetable has been jumpstarted (already feeling body aches and nausea tonight), and Charles concluded that I'll feel better faster. I hope so. Dr. Koon tweaked my nausea meds. Fingers crossed.

I got some info from Dr. Koon today.

- My abdominal "certainly a tumor" is in fact, a bruise. As I described the pain and how it had tapered off to a just tenderness in the area, he was really convinced that it was just an injury.
- The Lymph node concern is most likely the result of some type of ingrown hair. I mentioned that perhaps my DAYS of worrying about cancer recurrence seemed a little silly now, but he was kind enough to say that it happens a lot and it's always nice to get good news.
- My prognosis is more positive since the MMMT hasn't spread like we originally thought, although I will need to be monitored closely. He mentioned that it's likely that I'll need more chemo in the future. That

was sort of a bruising gut punch in itself, but I'll try not to be afraid of those bridges until I come to them. (And maybe then I'll be considered really "sick" and get the chemo bed.)

- My CA 125 a tumor marker blood test—has shown a decrease and that's good. It's not a super reliable diagnostic tool, but it is a source of information regarding the presence of certain kinds of cells. Other inflam-mations can trigger an elevated number, but it does give doctors some info determining need for further investigation. The normal range is 0 to 35. Before my surgery, my number was 76, and now it is a 14.

It's hard to walk into a place knowing that you're going to feel worse for weeks after you leave. I got a little emotional in the lab waiting area and the receptionist, Michelle, just came over and gave me the biggest hug and comforting reassurances.

The same emotional sobbing response happened when Dr. Koon's nurse asked me how I was doing. Megan attempted to nonchalantly grab a tissue for me. Unfortunately, as I had changed into my examination gown, I had folded up my underwear and put it on top of the only Kleenex box in the room. Sharing that info was just another dignity boost for me.

So, if you're keeping score at home—
Chemo treatments completed = 4
Chemo treatments remaining = 2
Irrational fears that turned out to be a concern = 0
Overly emotional = 2
Considered to be "sick" = -1
Side effects=Mach 3
Dignity=fair to partly cloudly

Yours 'til the bruise cruises,

Sarah

———

July 23, 2007—9:40pm

One of my most favorite moments ever was when Molly Carter (a black lab) would greet me after not seeing me for a while. It could be months, and her tail-wagging contortionist glee made feel great. How wonderful that another living thing was so HAPPY to see me!

For one reason or another (illness, conflict, etc) I had missed my Monday support group at Gilda's Club for the past three weeks. I almost got the same kind of welcome. And I don't even know these people's last names. I always benefit from our group. Tonight it was both ends of the spectrum. One member has died, and two others have recently been found to be cancer-free.

- There's fear.......of dying, of upcoming surgery, of a "tumor marker" blood test, of a first chemo session.
- There's doubt.......should I pay my annual credit card fee will I live long enough to use it? Can I keep from smoking? It's a moment at a time, not a day at a time for some. What will people think if I tell them I have cancer (You know, I urge people to tell and start playing the c cards.)
- There's hope....Maybe radiation is working, this chemo round has been better, I'm feeling more energetic, I'm exercising,
- There's laughter.......chemo brain moments, organized closets, aliases, family, and the weekly "worst thing a healthcare professional has said" contest. (I almost won with the "We save the beds for people who are sick," but "You're definitely going to die." was a clear winner.)

This round of chemo has been much less severe. I'm battling fatigue but much less nausea and aching. My mother arrived Friday and has given new meaning to waiting on me hand and foot (I love that!). I head up to Colorado to see the nieces and step-sibs on Thursday, and I'm sure MOLLY GLAD to be seeing them. (Did I mention the "hand and foot" part guys?)

And finally, I did have a happy 47th birthday on Saturday.

Yours 'til the cake mixes, (although mine was from scratch)

Sarah

—◆—

July 27, 2007—1:00pm

Flying the friendly skies.

Last night I flew on American Airlines from Dallas to Denver. Luckily, I was able to get an upgrade to First Class. (My sister says you're not spoiled if it's how is should be to begin with, btw).

The flight was bumpy, but everything's better in First, including the freshly baked chocolate chip cookies they serve near the end of the flight. Well, it's true, this batch was a little dry, but I braved through it, and polished mine off in no time.

Unfortunately, I got that little dry sliver of cookie caught in my throat and I had already finished my ginger ale. You know what I mean, it's hanging on just below where your Eustachian tube hits, and it's going to take some seriously throat clearing to take care of it.

I figure it's going to be better for everyone around if I head to the bathroom. I persevere and finally dislodge the offending cookie crumb. However, as I exit the lavatory, the two flight attendants are right there, and they think, "Oh, she's retching in there because she's in chemo." They are SOOOOO concerned. Are you okay? Do you need water? You're so brave. How can you even bring yourself to be flying? We've seen with a smile on your face through the whole trip (okay, I was watching THE OFFICE on the iPhone). You poor thing. What can we do?

Well, I can't really say, "*Take the cookies out two minutes earlier next time so they are soft and chewy.*" So I just smile and reassure them that I'm okay, and yes, chemo is hard, but I'm fine, and so on. I ALMOST felt guilty, but not quite.

I'm looking forward to the family gathering today. It's a cool spell in Colorado, so I timed it perfectly. The altitude is tougher on me and it's just noon and I've already had my first nap. Have a great weekend.

Yours 'til the cookie crumbles,

Sarah

July 31, 2007—5:36pm

> *Happiness is having a large, loving, caring, close-knit family in another city.* —George Burns

I got home last night (yes in First Class, no choking cookies) after a great weekend in Colorado. It was delightful to see my extended, blended family and friends. We laughed until we couldn't breathe, and I had a fabulous time tormenting the nieces.

My only disappointment is that I couldn't ever escape the fatigue. The altitude just made it worse, but luckily, I had my own air-conditioned suite at Chez Scooter, so naps were frequent. I'm tired of being tired, and I really look forward to that morning when I get to wake up and feel rested and ready to carpe diem again.

Of course, the other SLIGHT disappointment is that I wasn't able to hear ALL 13 (it's an unlucky number for a reason) songs on the Hannah Montana cd. Oh well, what can I say? I loved Bobby Sherman and the Partridge Family.

I have developed a slight cough that I can either blame on my niece Kaila or the millions of germs in the Denver airport. I'll get blood work done on Thursday, but I know that this is my low white blood cell count week. I have another week to gear up for chemo number five.

As we took off yesterday, I realized that I didn't see the mountains at all during the trip. I didn't really leave the house. Unfortunately, I was on the wrong side of the plane to catch a glimpse as we left. Still, I certainly got to do everything that I wanted to do. Thanks to Scott and Heidi for hosting and thanks to all of you who make me feel so loved this weekend and always.

Yours 'til the mountain peaks,

Sarah

PS—A picture from the wedding reception. What a grand time. Check it (and more photos) out on the SarahMerdian site at www.CarePages.com)

———

August 04, 2007—8:12am

> *When it's peach picking time in Georgia,*
> *Apple picking time in Tennessee,*
> *Cotton picking time in Mississippi,*
> *Everybody picks on me.*
> *When it's roundup time in Texas,*
> *The cowboys make whoopee,*
> *And way down in old Alabama,*
> *It's gal picking time for me.*
> — **Jimmy Rodgers**[2]

I've never asked "Why did cancer pick me?" I guess I figure "Why not me?"

Why not pick someone who has such wonderful support.

Why not someone who is constantly shown the humor in this dreadful disease?

Why not someone with insurance, and friends, and options, and a decently shaped bald head. (although I did just mention to Charles yesterday that I'm pretty tired of being bald. I miss my hair and eyelashes. Armpits I'm still fairly happy with them.)

I'm starting to explore the areas of complementary medicine, including massage, chiropractic, and acupuncture. These methods were suggested at a group meeting at Baylor, no less. I appreciate their open-mindedness. I think there's much to be said about the connections between life force energy and health and wellness. Just like the connections between prayer and strength and healing. Unseen, but certainly ever present.

I'm gearing up for Chemo 5 on Thursday. Christine comes down on Wednesday to provide some TLC and probably some distractions as well. Have a great weekend. As the Allmans would say, "Eat a peach."

Yours 'til the guitar picks,

Sarah

August 08, 2007—8:30am
What's in a number?

- The Jackson 5
- 5 senses
- A fifth of rum
- "Five golden rings"
- "The Figure 5 in Gold" painting (and a watch I own) by Charles Demuth
- 5 Civilized Tribes of Oklahoma (Choctaw, Chickasaw, Cherokee, Creek, and Seminole)
- Give me five
- 5 is slang for MI-5 in England (like 5-0 in Book 'em Danno)

- Five Easy Pieces
- The Fifth Element
- 9-to-5
- Fifth Avenue candy bar
- Cinco de Mayo
- Five Glorious Mysteries of the Rosary (see also Joyful, Luminous, and Sorrowful)
- Batting 5 hundred
- 5 o'clock shadow
- Take five
- V
- An Abraham Lincoln
- Maroon 5
- My favorite grade to teach.

Certainly, Chemo 5 can't be that scary.

Yours 'til I take the fifth,

Sarah

PS—Apologies to all the other fives that I've forgotten

August 11, 2007—9:39am

On my last day of chiropractic and acupuncture this Wednesday before chemo, Dr. Samadzada bounced into the examination room and asked, "*Are you ready for another step toward health and wellness?*" I, of course, wondered if anyone ever said anything but yes.

Well, Brent, please get the I-Told-You-Sos ready, because those treatments are really making this chemo round much better. I am still very fatigued, but I am not experiencing the dreadful aches and pains in my muscles and joints like before. This is usually worst day in the cycle, and today my discomforts are minimal. (However rest assured that I'm still milking it with Christine. The coffee and post chemo surprise rolls were fabu this morning.)

Of course I'm not discounting the thousands of prayers, upped anti-nausea meds, good karma, exercise, wonderful chemo nurse Ellen, and support that are all sent my way, but I think the chiro and accu has made me the big winner today. In fact, I feel good enough to send Christine on a little vicarious shopping therapy trip. (Sorry Joe).

Yours while there's breaks in the aches,

Sarah

August 13, 2007—1:06pm
This is a letter to my niece, Addison.

Dear Addie,

I wanted to say thank you for something that you said to me during my recent visit to Colorado. It's not about Hannah Montana, dancing, dominoes, or even looking through catalogues. No, it's what you told me about using a special strategy to feel safe. You mentioned that you imagined Violet's force field from "he Incredibles" It could surround you and keep things from bothering you so much.

Well, I have to tell you that I used that exact strategy during my chemotherapy session last week. The whole thing is still sort of scary to me....the needles, the sore hand, the weird ways the medicine makes me feel.....and I thought to myself that I just needed to imagine your (and Violet's) force field protecting me.

You said that it also helped knowing that your principal thought you were the greatest. Well, my nurse Ellen was just like that. Nice and caring people can help us through the toughest times, don't you think?

It also makes me think that if we can be a little brave this time, then we can be even more brave next time. Thanks again for sharing your strategies with me. You've learned in second grade what some people take a lifetime to understand. Big hug and a smooch,

Yours 'til Tia Sarita's la favorita,

Auntie Sarah

PS—Tell Brookers that my friend Christine was here this weekend, and she wears her hair flipped up in a clip just like Brooke.

———

August 15, 2007—8:58pm

> *I can no other answer make, but, thanks, and thanks.*
> **—William Shakespeare**

Today I attended a "Writing for Wellness" group at Baylor. Of course, what happens in WFW, stays in WFW (what did we say before that Vegas ad?), but I can share that in addition to topics on journaling and dealing with anger, loss, and other emotions, we discussed the idea of Gratitude Journals.

Some make a point to write daily and simply list five things they're thankful for that day. They revisit the entries periodically, especially during low points and times of frustration.

Well, needless to say, I have countless reasons for gratitude. This CarePage alone has brought me more comfort that you'll ever know. I'm thankful for the rides, meals, errands, cards, flowers, compassion, chores, prayers, healthcare professionals, laughs, and patience that have filled these past six months.

Sometimes I forget to be grateful for other things:

- All the times that the needle stick was just once
- Finally not feeling bad about what my body looks like (really, that one has taken a lifetime.)
- Enjoying good carbs
- My ever-increasing stamina and strength (not always forward, but always ahead)
- My tattoo
- Anticipated trips and events
- Did I say humor and laughter and laughter?
- iTunes
- The complete and unwavering knowledge that no matter what happens, it will be all right.

Yours 'til the grate's full,

Sarah

———

August 17, 2007—7:01am

When I was checking the MDA website for my upcoming appointment dates (Testing on September 19th, Seeing Dr. Coleman :-) and Dr. Butler on the 20th), I saw a news item on the dire need for blood donors. I remember the necessity of the 4+ units I received in the hospital. I can't give blood right now (although they take a little each week), so maybe you can. If you go to www.givelife.org, you can get local blood donation information. [picture]

Have a great weekend everyone. We're celebrating my Aunt Mary's 50th jubilee anniversary this weekend. Amen!

Yours 'til O's positive,

Sarah

———

August 21, 2007—10:18pm

The following post is from an email sent to me by none other than my dear Emily Tamblyn. Emily was a 5th grader in my class a million years ago, and she was just as fun and fearless way "back in the day." She currently lives in Chicago and is clearly one of the delights of the Windy City.

I saw Amanda's blood donation post (on CarePages), and I wanted to share Emily's experience as well. I laughed out loud. (Someone at last night's support group mentioned that she believed crying was part of 'getting the cancer' out of you. I'm pretty sure that mine is getting laughed out as well.)

I hate giving blood. Really I do. I faint kind of easily, which is embarrassing, and I always look down while they are taking out the needle. Bad move. But I'm an O-, universal donor, and so I keep giving blood, especially because there are a couple people in my family who have needed transfusions, so I feel like I have a responsibility to keep going.

But I tend to make blood-giving appointments, and then forget about them completely, because I really don't want to think about it. So last time I gave blood, which was nearly a year ago, they called to remind me the day before. I had forgotten all about it, of course, but I thought, hey, I'm going to be really smart and drink a TON of water before I give blood. So I chugged water like it was going out of style for a full day beforehand.

I went in, answered their questions and made myself comfy in a donation chair watching some Queen Latifah movie. I try to space out when they put the needle in, but I did notice that the tourniquet was very, very tight. I mentioned this to the phlebotomist, and she said that it wasn't a big deal, but it may take me longer to clot when I was finished giving. And sure enough when I was done and they took the needle out, I pressed the cotton ball to my arm, a little bit of blood squirted around it! Gross, sorry, I know. I felt instantly woozy, but I leaned back and talked myself out of it, focusing in on Queen Latifah.

A couple of minutes go by and I'm starting to feel human again. I decide that getting my apple juice and animal crackers will greatly improve the situation. I get up and walk over to the fridge no problem, but when I lean down the dizziness hits me. I feel myself start to black out, so I start moving fast back towards the beds and that is the last thing I remember.

Have you ever fainted, Sarah? If yes, then you know how it feels, like you are coming up slowly out of water. I could hear Queen Latifiah's voice, and I open my eyes and the nurse is sitting over me as I'm lying on the floor.

"Did I pass out?" I ask her.

"Yes."

"Did I fall?"

"No, I caught you. You are all right"

"Did I piss myself?"

Pause. "Yeah, sweetie, you did."

So it turns out that you lose all muscle control when you pass out, including bladder control. And my light blue linen pants were now teal. And the cute Puerto Rican nurse mopped up my mess, and I had to ride the train home in the ill-fitting sweatpants they loaned me.

I went home and cried for two hours, but now I think it's the funniest thing ever. I still haven't gone back to give blood. But I guess if you are brave enough to go through five grueling rounds of chemo, I can be brave enough to face the people who watched me wet myself again. Seems kind of minor relatively. I made an appt. for this Thursday.

Love you tons and missing you. *Em*

Sarah Merdian

August 23, 2007—5:02pm

Just so nice, they did it twice. I like to check on my weekly blood counts. Lately, I've been picking up a copy of the report after my Thursday group meeting at Baylor. That series ended last week, so I left a message for Megan, Dr. Koon's nurse, and asked her to give me a call today to share the results.

Well, Megan calls right when I'm at Lowe's deciding on a specific Whirlpool dishwasher. She's got good news and not so good news. The good news is that my CA 125 number is down to 7.80. (This is the tumor marker test. Normal is 0 to 35 and in the last nine weeks my numbers have been 14, 9, and now 7.8 much better than the pre-surgery 76). The not-so-good news is they forgot to include the orders for the CBC blood test and I need to go back down to Baylor and have my blood drawn again. At least they used the other arm. The fun just never stops.

I want to thank the unknown person who got a copy of Paul Brenner's *Buddha in the Waiting Room* into my hands. I am loving this book about a doctor's journey from his traditional medicine background to a new understanding about health and healing. He talks about the individuals who were a Buddha, or source of pure wisdom, in his life.

This observation struck a chord with me.

> *The whole body weeps when it is invaded. A person's wholeness has been compromised: physical and emotional. The psycho-social implications of surgery, radiation, and chemotherapy are enormous.*[3]

I am very aware that I am not simply a patient whose disease is being treated by medical personnel. My entire self is involved in healing. This perspective reaches beyond chemo and includes the support group, spiritual, nutritional, recreational and emotional components of my life as well as the complementary practices of chiropractic, meditation, acupuncture and massage. Hey, no wonder this cancer thing feels like a full time job.

To add to my gratitude journal—

- Thanks to SK for the world's—or maybe even the universe's—best tuna sandwich (haven't tried everything yet).
- Thanks and kudos to the blood donors.
- Thanks for all the posts and emails. They make my day.

And last but not least,

- Thanks to all who serve as a Buddha for me.

Yours 'til the whole body approaches,

Sarah

August 27, 2007—4:57pm

Winifred is our wonderful librarian at Peak Academy, and her daughter, Elizabeth, sent me the following email. Elizabeth is in training for the New York City Marathon, and she is running in support of the National Ovarian Cancer Coalition. She asked me to pass on donation info to all of you.

I'm happy to support her (although I'd be happy to give her a metro pass, so she doesn't have to run/walk those 26.2 miles. Really, the NY subway system is excellent, Elizabeth, and while the taxis are a little scary at times, they're certainly an option!)

Yours 'til the bus stops,

Sarah

August 29, 2007—5:14pm

> *If you find a path with no obstacles, it probably doesn't lead anywhere.* —Frank A. Clark

At the start of a recent acupuncture session, I told my doctor that I had been very emotional lately, and asked if he had any needles for that.

DR. "So, Sarah, you want to know if I have a needle for joy?"
Me: "Yes, in fact, I'll take two."

Upon reflection, I mentioned that I really did have a lot of joy already in my life, so maybe I only needed one needle. He inserted the needles like he always does, with one exception—a needle in my left elbow. I guess joy can be found anywhere.

I realize that a needle cannot take away my sense of loss and sadness due the fact that school started this week, and I'm not teaching. It's hard for me; it's the first time in 25 years that I'm not greeting a new class of 5th graders.

Yet, I've come to realize that once again, I have been given a path that is absolutely right for me right now. I'll be at Uplift working with curriculum materials and new teachers. I'm grateful for the opportunity even while I'm missing my own classroom.

What a blessing that every step of this journey has been along the exact right path. Never easy, but always right. Each and every doctor has played an indispensable role in my diagnosis and treatment. Each support person has provided and/or directed me to yet another beneficial resource, and I have encountered scores of wonderful people along the way. Tomorrow is my sixth and final chemo session. Down that road I go.

Yours 'til the last drop,

Sarah

PS—As for the needles in the elbows: Please do not try this at home.

August 30, 2007—8:46pm

All that glitters is not gold.

So, yesterday, I made a pre-chemo run to the grocery store and my cashier was Kimberly. I couldn't really make out the words on her cursive neck and upper arm tattoos, but I couldn't miss the bright pink glitter eye shadow. And, I'm talking craft project quality glitter.

I heard myself saying the words, '*Great eyeshadow*" Kimberly replied, "*Well you should wear some, too.*"

Now, I tell her that I should probably wait until my eyelashes and eyebrows grow back. I have so few eyebrow hairs left, that I'm thinking of naming each one. Well, I should have known better, because that one cancer reference starts the story.

"*Well, you know my dad had cancer. He really wasn't around when I was growing up, so I tracked him down, but he was headed to jail. He later called me from jail to tell me that they were letting him out because he was dying of brain cancer. Well, I told him that I had a surprise, too: My two-year-old son. They got to meet, but my dad died a week later. I did get a picture of them together though.*"

Well, I don't know the best response to that, so I just mentioned I'm beginning to believe everyone's life is touched by cancer in some way.

And then Kimberly said, "And she gave me my receipt. *Good luck on your cancer, and you saved $4.65 with your shopper card today.*" There you have it.

I'm home from chemo and I have to say that it ended with a whimper rather than a bang. I'm tired and have a headache and some early onset nausea. (usually the IV anti nausea meds last to the next day, but I have my meds at home, too.)

I can, however, add to my gratitude journal.

• My nurse Pam got me going with just one stick

- I did get the little room with the bed (much darker and quieter. I got to sleep)
- I got several encouraging and touching posts and emails. Thanks. You'll never know how much that means to me.
- This round of six chemo sessions is in the rearview mirror.

Yours 'til the eye shadows,

Sarah

———— ⌁ ————

September 01, 2007—9:58am

"My Writing for Wellness" leaders suggested "facing a doctor's visit and tests" as a prompt for writing.

FAREWELL, but not GOODBYE
My last chemo
My final chemo
My sixth chemo

This is more the end of a chapter than the final pages of a book.

The doctor MENTIONED that some patients are doing a once-a-month chemo for 12 months. Just Taxol every 4 weeks. A new chapter. PERHAPS another bald chapter, I guess. There MIGHT be radiation. It's only about 20 minutes, and it's everyday, but we DON'T know yet. A chapter from the cookbook? Your MDA doctor is the chemo expert. He'll look at your scans and tests, and you guys can decide what's best. I'll be here to help in anyway I can. Another chapter in three weeks.

Ah, I get it. This book is a mystery. Not so much a who-dun-it, but more of a labyrinth-filled, twists and turns, awake in the night, nail biting psychological thriller that I can't quite put down.

Yours 'til the book reports,

Sarah

PS—Chemo Day 3 update: Minimal body aches, mild headache, moderate nausea. Much better.

PPS—It is really September? Happy Labor Day to everyone!

September 02, 2007—3:10pm

Well it just goes to show you, I guess. I thought I had eluded the dreaded aches and pains of chemo. Yesterday, I just had the symptoms of a mild hangover (without the prerequisite carousing), but today, the proverbial chemo hammer has come down.

I am hesitant to describe the feelings, not because they're too gruesome to share, but rather that I'm vain enough to worry about how I am remembered. I have likened the deep and severe post-chemo aches in my hips to an overcooked chicken. You know, I feel like if I get up, the bone might just fall from my hip like the chicken bone does.

Here's the problem. A friend told me that now whenever he passes the rotisserie chickens at the store, he thinks of me and imagines my head on top of the chicken's body. That makes me think that I'm somehow trapped in the house of the mean next-door neighbor kid in Toy Story. (Maybe his name was Sid?)

So, I'm hanging in there with achy knees, arms, hips, and shoulders. Charles came to the rescue with some 7-Up and my anti-nausea meds are kicking in. Hopefully this phase will be over soon. I'm grateful for my two easy early days.

Yours 'til the side dishes,

Sarah

PS—And to think that some people say I "over think" things. Geez.

　　　　　　　　　　　　　　　　　Sarah Merdian

September 05, 2007—2:01pm

I'm emerging (at a snail's pace) from the chemo side effects. Yesterday I managed to get in a swim, and luckily for friends, I saved my daily cry time for the acupuncturist. (Yes, I did end up getting two joy needles.)

I was dead tired and achy last night. It's so strange to be in my nightgown and in bed before the sun goes down. (Maybe that evens out all those late college nights when the sun came up? Who knows? The Chicago boys will remember that ugly blue light.)

At my "Writing for Wellness" class today we discussed the idea of finding your "new normal" and one woman mentioned that sometimes she just has to accept that a condition is "my normal today." I like that idea. I know that the post-chemo song and dance is unpredictable, so if I can just sort of figure it out day-by-day that might be enough.

There's a chance that I might be starting back to work next week. I'll find out later and keep you posted. Until then, I'm working on hydration and rest. Who knew drinking water and sleeping could count as a to-do list, but they're both on mine!

Yours 'til the baby steps,

Sarah

September 06, 2007—9:11am

Just Peachy (apologies to Imelda). I just bought a new camera for my October trip to China. (How nice has it been to have a light at the end of the tunnel?) Cancer has unstamped my passport several times in 2007, and anticipating this trip has been a real boost.

Anyhoo, back to me. Charles and I were trying out the new camera and I was surprised to see my latest image. Here I am: Hair White and the Seven Brows (Crinkly, Sleepy, Stringy, Grumpy, Wiry, Hairy, and Doc). I'm starting to get this soft peach fuzz on my head. Who knows how this last round of chemo will affect it.

I've mentioned before that one of the blessings of my cancer is finally feeling okay about who I am physically. Getting the tattoo has been empowering. I have never worn my wig, and I do wear a few hats for sun protection. (This peach burns), but mainly, I feel very comfortable being bald in public.

How is it that we let too few or too many pounds, hairdos, hair-don'ts, zits, and/or wrinkles affect how we feel about our own worth as a person? (Sounds pretty preachy from a woman that doesn't even have a belly button, doesn't it!) Anyway, be happy with yourself. The rest of us love you already.

Yours 'til the hair's apparent,

Sarah

PS—Feeling stronger everyday. In fact, I was awake until after DARK last night. I'm off to swim and get my weekly blood work at Baylor.

September 08, 2007—5:49pm

Pride goeth before the fall. (Hmm, before the fall—that's early September right? Then I guess I'm right on schedule.)

LOVE YOUR LASHES

At the beginning of chemo, they suggested that I get a baking-soda toothpaste because other flavors, especially with breath fresheners, can contain alcohol which would anger my mouth sores. I've been using a peroxide-and-baking soda version WITHOUT INCIDENT until last Thursday. As I drew the bristles across the emerging ribbon of toothpaste, I inadvertently created a toothbrush catapult which, yep, you guessed it, flipped the paste with Olympic gold medal accuracy straight into my eye. Yes, eyelashes would have helped. You can't imagine how much it burned.

GRAVITY IS THE LAW

Today I was searching out a few bargains at the local bookstore. I was sitting on a little stool, and my head cocked sideways, so I could read the titles on the bottom clearance shelf. I had mentioned to the family of four next to me that I could scoot over. They said, "No problem." Liars. Needless to say, I was unprepared when Dad reached over me to grab a book from the top shelf and caused a neighboring top shelf hardback to fall right on my head. The book plummeted at an angle, so the lower right corner points could make direct contact. The folks were quite apologetic, and I reassured them that I knew it was an accident, and I did make it to the magazine section before I did actually start to cry. Luckily, it was a children's book, so rather than a goose egg, I have more of a quail egg.

STRETCH OF THE IMAGINATION

Dr. Samadzada, my chiro and acupuncturist, has given me some stretching exercises. It's a copied packet from *The Chiropractic Handbook for Patients* and each exercise has a description and a drawing of a woman who appears to have been an extra in Olivia Newton-John's "Let's Get Physical" video because, and I do not lie, she is wearing a leotard AND a head sweatband. The good doctor wants me to do each exercise once a day for 12 repetitions. I had no problem with the torso side bends, the torso twist, the neck rotation and the neck bends. However, the floor exercises are another matter.

First of all, there's getting on the floor. I was on my back trying to do the "knee to the forehead" maneuver. Okay, even placing both hands behind one thigh to bring it up caused my knee to make sounds usually only heard in a Rice Krispies commercial. I'm beginning to wonder if he really meant "12 repetitions per week".

We'll not even discuss the "midwives only" image created by one "both knees to the forehead" attempt.

Now we move onto the knees for the torso stretch and the, yes, donkey kicks. One would think that having the enlarged ovaries as well as the cumbersome uterus and other pelvic residents removed would "lighten up the load" on my knees, but no such luck. I mean, forget the floor. I can barely get in one good torso stretch ON MY SLEEP NUMBER BED. Clearly, this exercise is more of the 12 repetitions per year sort of thing. I guess we all start somewhere.

All I can say is if you happen to see a large proud bald woman with a knot on her head and a patch over her right eye crawling down Gaston Avenue to the chiropractor's office next Tuesday, please be sure to honk and wave.

Yours 'til the accident's prone,

Sarah

———

September 12, 2007—10:55pm

My "one week until your appointment" reminder email from M. D. Anderson came today. It's hard to believe that I'm through with my treatment. I've struggled with how to approach learning the results of my upcoming tests. A guy from my support group sees it as *"I've finished all my courses, now I need to see if I get my diploma."* I don't think that will work for me.

I also cannot allow myself to worry anxiously about the "what ifs". What if a tumor has grown? What if cancer has spread to other areas? What if I'm dying soon? Even if none of these conditions exist, I'll still have more tests in upcoming months. I can't live a life that is filled with such anxiety between benchmarks. I'm afraid that it wouldn't really be living my life, it would be time spent fearing cancer.

I have decided that I can only approach it as part of a process. I'll go to Houston and find out what our efforts and I do mean our efforts, including everyone that has held me dear in their hearts and prayers as well as my healthcare providers and treatment—have accomplished so far. And then, we'll go from there.

Yesterday, as the acupuncture needles were being inserted, I asked Dr. Samadzada what wisdom he had to share with me. He told me we should do the little thing that we could do TODAY to better others. I think it's a wise approach to take with ourselves as well.

Yours 'til today's the present,

Sarah

PS—Yes, I'm also THRILLED that I'm going to be seeing my Dr. Coleman.

———

September 16, 2007—5:41pm

Somehow it seems to fit. The week when I have my lowest blood cell counts and feel so fatigued is the same week that someone in my neighborhood gets…………a rooster. This rooster greets the sun each morning with a healthy crow, but apparently he must have some sort of ADD because it sounds like he's surprised by the sun's presence over and over and over throughout the day. Anyone have a good recipe for coq au vin?

I started doing some curriculum work last week and as my chiropractor was eager to tell me, sitting at the dining room table for extended hours is not so good for the lower back. It was nice to be productive and get some hours in however. I've been invited to teach a math lesson in a 5th grade class next Tuesday. I know over half of the kids, and I'm thrilled.

I head down to Houston on Wednesday, and I'll have blood work, chest x-rays, and a CAT scan done. I'll meet with Dr. Coleman on Thursday. I continue to do my best to keep from fear and worry about all of this. I remind myself that it's just the next thing, and I can and will handle whatever comes. I remember

Dr. High, the cardiologist that cleared me for surgery, saying, *"Sometimes we open the door to fear, and nothing's there."* We shall see. I'll keep everyone posted on my results.

Yours 'til cat scans,

Sarah

September 20, 2007—5:30pm

THE SCAN IS CLEAR! NO CANCER IS VISIBLE! WOW.

More details to follow, but I wanted to share the great news. Thanks again for the wonderful support. I feel like this has been a group effort. And yes, Dr. Coleman did take a picture of my tattoo with HIS iPhone to share at his lectures.

Yours while we're in the "no",

Sarah

September 24, 2007—11:15am

There's no quick way to sum up my two days at M.D. Anderson. Okay, you've been warned.

The first day was testing, and I'll limit it to the highlights, and I do use the word "highlights" with sarcasm.

- Shaky Sara, the new trainee, takes my blood.
- Mother swears it won't be humid and then we hike down the block to the radiology building. Sweaty, party of one. (Oh, turns out there's a lovely shuttle van that makes the rounds every 15 minutes.)
- The CT tech informs me that I can select from berry, banana, apple, and original flavor barium "smoothies",

  Sarah Merdian

but then I'm informed that the required barium enema does not have the same choices. He quickly redirects the conversation with a, "*So, what's up with all the tattoos?*" and then proceeds to call me "INF" for the rest of the day.

- The sweet young thing that administers the BE says, "*Since I'm giving you this, we should probably be on a first name basis. I'm Elizabeth.*" God love ya, Elizabeth.
- My CT session ends with 4 people around me discussing their ideas for possible tattoos and then I head back to the waiting area where I find two strangers wearing my INF buttons. Looks like Mother has made some new friends.

All throughout the day, the tension of waiting, waiting, waiting, was exhausting, but I still had the feeling that no matter what the results, everything was going to be okay. The feeling is somewhat like an ocean wave that as it hits the shore, washes away the doubt that nags at me in the back of my mind.

The next morning's trip to Dr. Butler revealed the following:

- He's VERY proud of his work and thinks my incision looks great.
- He told me that they almost lost me on the table. (That was news to me. I thanked him once again for all of his efforts.)
- In addition to the regular dignity-filled naked-against-the-blue-wall photographs, I was instructed to raise my hands over my head and arch my back. Don't try to conjure up an image. Sometimes life is just surreal.
- The CT scan revealed that I have a seroma which is a collection of fluid that often occurs after plastic surgery.

It's not painful or dangerous and my body may later absorb the fluid. Dr. Butler's recommendation (and he knows seromas, in fact he's written a couple papers on the topic Ooo la la) was to leave it alone. He can drain it with a syringe later if it starts to bother me.

And then I got to see my Dr. Coleman. After hugging me in the hallway, he later entered my room and noticed my iPhone. Well, of course, we had to discuss that first. It's nice to know that we have priorities while I'm on my back ready for my exam.

Then, it turns out that my "two" cancers have slipped his mind, and he's confused and concerned, and as he's gloved for my exam, and then searching the computer for my path report, he turns his head around and mentions, "*Oh yeah, your scan was clear. No cancer is visible.*" Have I mentioned surreal yet?

The rest of the visit was sort of a discussion of options. Since monthly lower dosage chemo has not proven to prevent recurrence or increase longevity, I've opted to do my best to live my life and be as healthy as I can. I'll go in for a scan in three months, and then we'll go from there.

Before I left, Dr. Coleman did want to take a picture of my tattoo. He also wants a tee shirt of the design to wear at lectures. I was sitting still and straight-faced so he could take the photo, but he was trying to get an angle shot of my face as well. "*Come on, show me some love.*" And he snapped away as I was laughing.

So, the shift from cancer patient to cancer survivor occurs in a subtle instant, and I'm not quite sure I'm absorbing all of it yet. I'm not certain what I'm supposed to be learning from all of this, but I'll keep looking and listening.

I spent a great weekend with friends, and this week, I'm diving into curriculum work. No rest for the weary. No complaints from the blessed.

Yours 'til the next wave,

Sarah

September 30, 2007—9:35am

It's been 10 days since I found out about my clear scans. Of course, it's wonderful news and I've so appreciated the multitude of supportive responses from everyone. Yet, I've had this less than ecstatic feeling deep down inside and more of a feeling of being overwhelmed with the news.

I've heard over and over in my support group that a sort of depression often sneaks in when treatment is over. Cancer, and doctors, and procedures, and holding on, and getting through it become your full time job, and then poof, that's gone, and you're left wondering and trying to find your new "new normal." Your life just doesn't go back to how it was the day before you found out you had cancer.

Last night, dear Ann Casey, helped me understand what's going on with me. I've spent the last eight months establishing within myself a belief that my worth, my satisfaction, my dreams, my determination, my love, my spirit, my happiness, and really, my life all had meaning and purpose that were SEPARATE from cancer. I had cancer, but cancer could not have me.

As we were driving from MDA to the airport, I told Mother that I felt there was something that I was supposed to be learning from all of this, but I couldn't figure out what it was. I think I'm seeing a glimpse.

If we can really believe that in any given moment, the person we are is worthy of love, life, happiness, hope, acceptance, respect, and laughter, (and I truly believe that God wants us to feel that way), then nothing can take that away. It's a state of peace that exists with or without cancer. (We've all had these A-HA moments. I guess this is sort of a Psalm 23 moment for me.) So all in all, I am thrilled and grateful that my tests showed no cancer. I'm just realizing that cancer, or lack thereof, has little power over who I truly am. I'll feel the same way when I have tests done in December. I'm living my life and taking things as they come.

I continue to make progress on my stamina, and I've been working A LOT lately. I have learned that mentioning, "*Well now I can stop trying to pick out songs for my funeral.*" is an awkward response to an inquiry about how I'm feeling. Sorry DC (but in my defense, I mentioned this to my sister and she has threatened Red Hot Chili Peppers and Love Rollercoaster. See, I knew to think about it.)

I'm having a C.H.I.L.I. (Cancer Has Its Limitations, Indeed) Party next Friday to celebrate and thank everyone for their support. If you're in the neighborhood, stop by for a beer or a bowl or at least a hug. My white peach fuzz feels just like a puppy, and you're free to give it a rub for luck.

Yours 'til the moments notice,

Sarah

◦

October 12, 2007—6:41pm

> *Remember, you are no sicker the day of diagnosis than you were the day before.*
> **—Vickie Girard**
> *There's No Place Like Hope*

I would venture that you're also no healthier the day of a good report than you were the day before. Don't get me wrong. I'm thrilled at my clear scan news. I'm just realizing that cancer is not a switch that flips on and off.

I am getting stronger. I have good days and not-so-good days when it comes to fatigue. I have a tendency to feel better then overdo it a little. Maybe most of us are like that anyway.

I'm been doing loads of curriculum work, and I threw a C.H.I.L.I. (Cancer Has Its Limitations, Indeed) Party last Friday. Over 50 friends—from college, school, and support groups—came to celebrate. It was a perfect evening even though we ran out of Fritos fairly early. (It's not a chili pie without Fritos!).

My hair is growing and I sort of have a 5 o'clock shadow for eyebrows. I tried to put some mascara on my stubbly little eyelashes, but after poking myself in the eye twice, I decided that I needed to wait another millimeter or two. The lady at our local Thai restaurant told me that my eyes are bright, so she knows that I'm healthy and have a good soul. Good to know.

I guess this next week will be the true test of my recovery. In a few hours I'm getting on a plane to Hong Kong. I'll be gone a little over a week. I'll also spend a couple days in Beijing, so plan on a GREAT WALL Christmas card photo this year!

I saw my chiropractor today, and he suggested that while I was in China that I should partake in massage, green tea, and acupuncture and qigong exercises in public parks. I'm not quite sure that 1.3 billion people need to see me exercising quite yet. I do feel comfortable drinking tea in public, however, and I'm always game for a massage.

Looking forward to this trip has really been a "light at the end of the tunnel" for me. Trips to Thailand and Italy were scrapped this year because of my condition. It's nice to know that chemo doesn't affect wanderlust. Our flight leaves at 10 pm on Friday, and we arrive in HK at 10:00am on SUNDAY. I know there's a time difference figured into that, but whew, that seems like a long time. I figure it has to be better than being in ICU, right?

Happy trails to all of you.

Yours 'til the Peking ducks,

Sarah

October 17, 2007—09:51am

It's almost 8 months to the day since Dr. Koon mentioned that I probably had six months to live if I didn't do anything and less than 2 years if I had surgery and chemo. And here I am Standing on the Great Wall of China. Huffing and puffing (and that's after taking the cable car....remember that fear of heights?)

The Wall seems to be a perfect example of what the human spirit can accomplish. We leave Beijing tomorrow, and head back to Hong Kong.

Yours 'til the tea leaves,

Sarah

October 26, 2007—7:17am

Well, the sleeping portion of the jet lag hasn't really settled yet. I was up at 3:00am this morning (even before the rooster). I bet I can squeeze in a nap before my 25th reunion dinner at the University of Dallas this evening. I look forward to laughing with old friends (and I do mean old).

We visited Beijing, Shenzhen, and Hong Kong. Highlights included the Great Wall, the Forbidden City, the Temple of Heaven, Hong Kong harbor, and the Gemmy factory tour.

The trip was very tiring for me, indeed, but I can't tell you how thrilling it was to be smack dab in the moment and feeling like I was living MY life. Loads of laughs, mountains of memories, and a sense of self stay with me. Three weeks until we head to Prague. I can't wait.

Yours 'til the pass ports,

Sarah

October 30, 2007—6:38pm

> *Some people think it's holding on that makes one strong sometimes it's letting go.*
> —Sylvia Robinson

  Sarah Merdian

I'm having a hard time finding some balance between hope and the present. Currently, I feel like I'm living in a window of opportunity. I had a clear scan in September, and I will have my next scan around Christmas. It's almost like I feel that I have to cram as much "living" as possible in this three-month time frame because I don't know what will come next. The irony is that we never ever really know what's coming next.

Yet that realization doesn't keep my mind from wandering. My dear goddaughter Lauren's wedding is just days after my next benchmark. I find myself worrying about how I can keep bad news from affecting that big day (especially since I have the worst poker face.) It troubles me that I let myself get so wrapped up in the unknown.

And my wonderful Charles, who is so patient during my irrational rants, wonders why I would ever consider such secrecy since it would limit the support I would get from those around me. I keep trying to tell him that I realize they're called "irrational fears" for a reason. God love him.

Do I think that preparing myself will lessen the potential blow? I hear in my support group that it's very typical for a cancer survivor to struggle with the fear of recurrence. I'm not sure that what I'm feeling is fear of cancer. I seem to be at peace in that regard. If cancer is present, then I'll need to start a new round of treatment—and I am okay with that. I'm willing and ready to fight the good fight as long as I can.

I just can't seem to shake the feeling that even though I don't have cancer, cancer still has a hold on me. The only thing that I can figure is that I'm afraid that I'm not living my life to the fullest. Sure, the China and Prague trips are part of grabbing the gusto, but I find myself forgetting birthdays, not keeping in touch with loved ones, and feeling precious time slip through my fingers. I seem to be focusing on what's missing rather than what's present, and I know that's not healthy thinking. So there you have it. Who knew that getting through treatment would not be quite the same as getting past it all?

Please don't worry I am really doing okay. I'm busy working, and I'm seeing steady improvement in stamina, especially in my swimming. I know that there are always bumps in the road, and I'm getting better at handling those things that I cannot control. I am reminded of the Serenity Prayer.

"God grant me the serenity to accept the things I cannot change; the courage to change the things I can; and the wisdom to know the difference."

And as Seinfeld's George Constanza would say, "Serenity, now!"

Yours 'til I'm not present "tense",

Sarah

PS—Mary, the present "tense" means nervous about present, not a wish to be past tense.

PPS—Happy Halloween. I simply had to post the trick-or-treat version of our picture.

November 04, 2007—8:43am

> *You can't always get what you want, but if you try sometimes you might find, you get what you need.*
> —M. Jagger & K. Richards[4]

Okay, this isn't the first time that I've found a parallel life lesson in a Rolling Stones song. (Let's be glad it wasn't "Sympathy for the Devil", right?)

I've gotten loads of response from my last posting. Thanks for your care and concern. Some of you seem quite worried about me. Please rest assured that I am okay. I'm so lucky to have a venue to honestly voice my thoughts, doubts, and joys. It's just part of this process.

In the week since my last update, two resources have found their way into my hands. First, a friend dropped off some CURE magazines. I had gotten a subscription last summer, but these were from the previous year. Well of course, one of the issues is called the SURVIVORS ISSUE. Several great articles, especially "Taking Control: Cancer survivors deal with fear," really hit home.

The second jewel has been sitting on my nightstand for over three months. I received a packet of information at my first Baylor lecture series. I remember thinking that cancer generates a ton of paper, and slid the folder and its thick contents onto the nightstand shelf.

Yesterday, I was looking for something else (you can't always get what you want), and I found that folder and the publication called "Life After Cancer Treatment" (you get what you need.). It's a book put out by......you'll never guess.........The U. S. Department of Health and Human Services. The book is a wonderful resource. I found much comfort in reading passages that reflect my exact feelings. A particular quote rang true. "As long as I was in treatment, I was killing the cancer. [After treatment} I was waiting for the other shoe to fall." —Judy, 45

I found another good reminder as I was reading last night. If we can find a way to express our feelings, whether in speech, art, or writing, then it's easier for us to deal with the feelings. We can get through them and maybe even let go.

I've spoken before about fighting an invisible dragon. I'm thankful to have an opportunity to face these feelings here. Your support means the world to me. I'd never be this far along without it.

The weather is glorious in Dallas, and I really enjoyed my extra hour of sleep last night. We leave for Prague in less than two weeks. Life is never perfect, but life is good.

(As they say in the magazine business)
Yours 'til the next issue,

Sarah

November 10, 2007—1:44pm

Squeeze Play One way that I can tell that I'm gaining strength and stamina is my swimming. I'm getting in three days every week, and I'm currently swimming twice as much as I did post surgery. (Still not as much as pre-surgery, but I'm getting there.)

I've NEVER been one to actually wear OUT a swimsuit, but it actually does happen. The chemicals must weaken the fabric because after a few months, the suit begins to deteriorate. I've recently had to say farewell to my favorite one-piece suit: a geometric print that really complemented my compass tattoo.

Big girls have long been fans of swim skirts, but I'm really enjoying the swim shorts. I also believe that wearing them constitutes a type of community service, and I'm pretty sure that I might be eligible for a grant from the Cottage Cheese Foundation if I agree to keep these thighs under wraps. So even with the one piece, I toss on the swim shorts. Everyone's happy.

Last summer, I got an H2O waterproof case and headphone set for my iPod. It's fabulous. I made a special playlist of songs that would get my heart rate and swim fins moving. However, even on shuffle, one can only listen to P!nk's "Get the Party Started" and Rocky Horror's "Time Warp" for just so many swim sessions before one longs for more variety.

Hey, no problem. I've got 3500+ songs on my iPod. I'll just put it on random and enjoy a wider collection. Usually, I'm pleasantly surprised, but every once-in-while, a swim session buzz kill like Johnny Mathis' "Chances Are," comes on and I need to quickly FF to the next song.

The H_2O case has a raised click wheel that activates the safe and dry ipod controls. It only takes the press of a button to skip to the next song. Unfortunately, the only place that I can safely "store" the bulky case is….you guessed it….down the back of my swim shorts. The headphones connect behind the neck and the cord runs down my back to the case.

Sarah Merdian

Sure, it's a little awkward to reach behind one's....
uhm...behind, and press a button when you're swimming.
However, it was MUCH easier when I was still wearing the one
piece suit and the swim shorts OVER that suit. The ipod fit nicely
between the two suits. Now, it's just me and the junk in my trunks,
so to speak. One would guess that my ample derriere would provide
almost a shelf like structure for the case, but no, it slides all around,
and I'm not even going to guess what I must look like when I go
to press the button.

My only hope right now, is that I either get a new one piece
(family....Christmas idea) or that my gluteus maximus muscles
strengthen from the swimming (butt of an athlete to match my
heart?) and I will soon be able to skip to the next song with just a
buttocks contraction. A girl can dream.

Yours 'til I turn the other cheek,

Sarah

November 15, 2007—7:58pm

> *When I started counting my blessings, my whole*
> *life turned around.*   —Willie Nelson

We all have so much for which we are thankful. We remember
to express gratitude for our family and friends as well as for our
blessings and joys. Of course, this year has reminded me to be extra
thankful for health and support. In addition, I've been surprised at
the many things that I never realized I would be SO grateful, so
thankful, for having. Some of these weren't missed until they were
gone. I never dreamed some other things would even matter to me.
Finally, I'm so fortunate to have never been without the others.

Unexpected Gratitude **A personal A to Z**

A = Air Flare....my own angel flight
B = Blue Cross/ Blue Shield
C = CarePage and Chiropractor and yes, CANCER
D = Drains
E = Epidural
F = Flowerpots on my porch
G = Gilda's Club
H = Hair
I = iPhone, iPod, & iTunes
J = Job
K = Knowing
L = Letting go
M = Mobility
N =Nose hairs
O = Oncologists
P = Phlebotomists
Q = Quiet
R = Recliner
S = Sleep number bed
T = Tupperware
U = Unwavering belief that it's all okay
V = Veins
W = Water
X = X-rays & medical technology
Y = You (yes, you)
Z = Zofran (anti-nausea drug)

Here's to appreciation and savoring and believing and hoping and grace. As they say in the Czech Republic, "Na zdravi!" (to your health). I wish everyone a wonderful and happy Thanksgiving. I am beyond grateful.

Sarah Merdian

Yours 'til Plymouth Rocks,

Sarah

—◦—

November 28, 2007—8:20am

> *Anyone who keeps the ability to see beauty never*
> *grows old* —**Franz Kafka.**

I have experienced feeling so small when I'm next to the ocean. Prague, which is so rich with its thousand+ years of history, makes me feel so young and filled with wide-eyed wonder.

The intricate art nouveau ornamentation of buildings, the mixture of architectural styles, the incredible statues, and the attention to detail create a beautifully breath-taking city. Walking the uneven cobblestone streets brings to mind the countless others who have gone before me. I am one in so many.

Spending Thanksgiving week (in a year where I have SO MUCH to be thankful for) in Prague was a treat. Laughter and music, cold and warmth, sleep and sights, friends and friends.

Now, I must admit, I'm not really sold on the flying "coach" part, but I'm not expecting any sympathy. Hope you had a wonderful holiday.

Yours 'til the Czech clears,

Sarah

—◦—

December 05, 2007—6:25pm

In third grade, all I really wanted for Christmas was an Easybake Oven. Baking cupcakes with a light bulb is a silly thing, but my fingers were crossed.

At our house, there were a few Christmas rules. First, people wrapped gifts and put them under the tree; Santa left your unwrapped gifts in the family room where you put your stocking.

Secondly, kids were NOT allowed to get their presents without the parents. Finally, under no circumstances could we wake up parents before 6:00am on Christmas morning.

This Christmas Eve Mother had a horrible flu, so Daddy was sleeping on the couch. This affected the placement of the stockings for Santa. I settled for the area just past the couch where an antique student desk folded out as an end table.

I woke up around 3:00am and watched the minute hand painfully tick off the LONGEST minutes that a person has ever had to endure. Clearly, I would not live to 6:00am.

It couldn't really matter if I just quietly went into the family room to "check" on the Easybake Oven. I wasn't going to play with it. Where's the harm in that?

I'm sure my heartbeat was louder than my father's snores. I took a deep breath and tiptoed past the couch. My stocking area was just inches away from his head, but I couldn't make out anything in the dark. I put my hands out in front of me and began to gently feel the presents. I found my stocking, all bulgy and wonderful. As I fumbled around in the dark, my father stirred. I froze as he rolled over on the couch. I waited, paralyzed, until I heard the rhythmic breathing once again.

Back on task, I could feel clothes, and books, and then….why, yes…..I could feel the knobs of the Easybake Oven. I was ecstatic! I was destined to bake a birthday cake for the Baby Jesus after all! Life was sweet. I was glowing.

But the Easybake Oven was actually a clock radio……..a clock radio that was plugged in……..a clock radio that was plugged in just inches away from my father's head, and I was turning the knobs. As the distinctive not-quite-tuned-in AM radio music BLARED, my father sat up straight, albeit befuddled, as I did a record breaking sprint to my bedroom.

Christmas was ruined. I had done the unthinkable. I envisioned my limp empty stocking in the desolate giftless area of our family room. There would be no light bulb cake for our dear Savior this year. There would be no Christmas for me.

It was an ETERNITY until 6:00am and I held back until my sister came to get me. My best acting performance was required. I needed to "act" like a child who might possibly deserve something besides lumps of coal. I was trying to decide on the best facial expression for "totally-innocent-shock-and confusion." Upturned palms were needed and darting glances and a bewildered shaking of the head. It was showtime!

Of course, my presents were all there, and my stocking was overflowing. The Easybake Oven turned out to be a wrapped gift under the tree, and it wasn't long before I felt like a talented Betty Crocker.

Later that day, my father mentioned that Santa must have set the clock radio for the wrong time zone because it went off in the middle of the night. I remember shrugging in that nonchalant way that comes so naturally to all third grade delinquents.

My father taught me many things. Sometimes by what he said, but more often by what he did. He believed that one should always have something to look forward to doing. He believed that not trying was worse than trying and failing. He believed that happiness was something that everyone deserved. He believed in laughter. He believed in me.

My father died 9 years ago today. I miss him now just as much as I did then, but I am more able to truly enjoy his memory these days. He will always remain a part of me. Warmth replacing pain is the gift that time brings us.

I hope your holiday season is filled with countless happy moments that will become tomorrow's memories.

Yours 'til the radio stations,

Sarah

December 15, 2007—1:07pm

I've seen several end-of-the-year programs that highlight songs, scandals, and significant moments from 2007. Here are my FIVE most memorable lines of 2007 (fully annotated for your enjoyment).

> **Without treatment, you might have 6 months to live. With treatment, probably less than 2 years.**

Dr. Koon said this when I was expecting to hear about the next week's surgery. I don't fault Dr. Koon; he's a good guy, and I had asked him to be straight with me. He was using known information and statistics. I now realize that he just didn't know me, and I'm stubborn enough not to take something like this at face value. I do plan to get my next tattoo on February 15, 2009. It will be 2 years. You can come, too.

> **Oh, I'm not good at this. Start over.**

These words came from my mother. Picture this: I'm in ICU on a ventilator and my hands are tied to the bedrails. The only way I can communicate with my mother is by tracing letters in her hand. I'm boiling hot. I want her to wipe my head with the cool rag. I spell out R-A-G, and she says, "rag". I nod. I look up, hoping that she'll understand that I mean my forehead. She guesses the overhead light and then the pillow (why those things need a rag, I'll never know). I shake my head no. I start to spell out "head", and she repeats the letters as I trace them. "H…..E….A….C? no, L?, no, R?. Oh, I'm not good at this, Start over." Now think about it; this is a woman who does the crossword puzzle in PEN. My sister wanted to know why I didn't just pinch her hand the next time.

> **We usually save the beds for people who are sick.**

  Sarah Merdian

I heard this from the chemo nurse. I had asked to use one of the many empty beds rather than the recliner because the Benadryl IV made me drowsy. The beds were in little rooms that were darker and quieter. I remember thinking, "Hey, wait a minute. Doesn't the fact that I'm in chemo count as being SICK?"

It's not a problem. I'll take care of it.

Calmly stated by Karen Papania, a former college roommate, who stayed with me for a few days during my convalescence. I woke up in the middle of the night and the sheets were wet. One of my remaining drains had come loose, and I was seriously leaking. I was pressing some tissues up against the hole in my abdomen as I held my remaining drains and tried to get to the tv room where freshly laundered towels were folded on the table.

Gravity and walking just made the flow greater. Bodily fluid was dripping down my legs and onto the floor. I grabbed the towels: one to replace the soaked tissues and one to try to mop up the already sticky substance on the floor. Bending over was excruciating and I tried to use my foot with the towel, but that just increased the stream. I was scared and repulsed and embarrassed and crying. I gave up and just climbed back into my cold and wet bed.

The next morning when Karen came downstairs, she was unflappable. She did the laundry, mopped the floor, and never batted an eye.

Ma'am, there's something metal in your bag.

The x-ray checkpoint security technician at the Hong Kong International Airport spoke these words. I figured she was talking about my metal glasses case. It was something else.

I reached into my purse, and my hand felt the object. Yes, Dan Flaherty had put a knife in my purse. A dirty pointy table knife from the hotel. Dan has spent the last 25+ years putting things in my purse. You'd think I'd learn. You'd think that he would think.

As I pulled the knife out of the bag and sputtered, "It's not mine." (Well, ma'am, it is in YOUR BAG), I felt a familiar warmth spread through my chest. It was the same feeling that I had when I was diagnosed with cancer.

They confiscated the knife and finally let me go. We were already on board the plane when I finally spoke to Dan. He laughingly asked, "Why didn't you tell them that you had it to cut the kiwi?" Kiwi? Now I was smuggling agricultural products into Taiwan?

And here comes 2008.

Yours 'til the memory fades,

Sarah

December 19, 2007—4:41pm

I don't have everyone's mailing address, but I did want to share my Christmas letter and photo with you all. (For many of you, this should look vaguely familiar....)

Yours 'til the holly branches,

Sarah

> *Health is a state of complete physical, mental and social well-being, and not merely the absence of disease or infirmity.*
> **—World Health Organization, 1948**

Dear Friends and Family,

Ah, health—clearly noticed when absent, unable to be purchased, and certainly a most treasured gift. Health is the product of balance, support, and grace. I am so appreciative of all the support you've provided me during this difficult year. So many factors are out of our control; let's choose to focus our energy and efforts where we can do the most good.

Seek balance.
Eat to live.
Realize that you are worth your own time.
Laugh more.
Pray for others.
Pray for yourself.
Stay in touch.
Choose.
Stretch your body and your mind.
Accept yourself.
Hold on.
Let go.

Wishing you health and happiness in the coming year,

Sarah

<hr>

December 24, 2007—10:04am

Monica, my favorite sister, returned home last night. She has to work today, but she was able to spend the weekend with us in Houston. We had our family Christmas on Sunday morning. We don't get up at 6:00am for it anymore.

Monica lamented that I hadn't shared the entire easy bake oven story. She recalls that I later used the EBO to bake mud pies and then forced her to eat them. "They're chocolate. If you don't like chocolate, then no one will like YOU." I have no memory of such a thing.

I almost remember switching out my Chiclets with Ex-Lax gum. (She shouldn't be a thief). I might recall mentioning that glowing end of the car lighter "tickled" and maybe I have a blurry memory of forcing her to drink my iced tea that she and her friend Nancy had spiked with vinegar. (There's a stealth move for you.) I definitely remember suggesting the "Let's see who can hit softest for a nickel" game and having her go first. She was nearly 25 cents richer before she caught on.

I have a friend who has said, "If I knew my brother was going to be so successful, I would have been a lot nicer to him growing up." I wonder if I would have been different had I known what a great support Monica would be during my battle with cancer. Hmm, probably……..not.

Thank goodness family loves us for who we are and in spite of who we've been.

Hope your holidays are going well.

Yours 'til it's all relative,

Sarah

❦

December 27, 2007—9:47pm

> **Fall seven times: stand up eight.**
> **—Japanese Proverb**

Today's news from Dr. Coleman was not what I had hoped. My CT scan showed a lymphatic area that has grown from 2cm to 2.5cm, and my CA-125 number has gone from 16 to 30. These are indicators for cancer recurrence.

I will have two or three cycles of treatment in Dallas with a medication called DOXIL, an intravenous chemotherapy that is often used for ovarian cancer recurrence. The treatment is once every four weeks, and the side effects are different (probably no hair loss, but possible rashes on my feet and hands as well as mouth sores). I plan on seeing Dr. Koon next week, so I can get started as soon as possible.

I can't express how much I appreciate Dr. Coleman. First and foremost, I feel so comfortable that he is treating ME and not just a disease. Additionally, MD Anderson's approach to cancer feels less like a death sentence and more like on-going problem solving. We'll try this treatment, and go from there.

There is much in my heart that I can't really articulate right now. I need to pack and get ready to leave tomorrow morning for Lauren and Christian's wedding. That's my priority.

This week I saw a Smithsonian magazine that listed "28 Places to See Before You Die" (I have seen 9 of them), and I saw a preview for a new movie, "The Bucket List" where Jack Nicholson and Morgan Freeman make a list of things to do before they "kick the bucket". I'm not ready to make such lists for myself. I am not willing to give up.

It was so sweet to see Dr. Coleman wearing my INF button. I really feel that way. I'm not finished. Fall seven times, stand up eight. I appreciate your continued prayers for strength and patience (and feel free to throw in wisdom as well.)

Yours 'til the kick stands,

Sarah

January 01, 2008—11:43am

2007—It's a wrap.

I received a lovely cotton blanket for Christmas, and I just took it out of the dryer. It was such a comfort to wrap its warmth around me on this chilly New Year's morning. I've been blessed to have been wrapped up and surrounded by such wonderful love and support during this past year. I thank you all who have visited my

CarePage over 1400 times this year. I get so much from reading your messages and emails.

The image of wrapping it up brings thoughts of a finalization, completion, or ending. Especially during the holiday season, wrapping also summons the idea of unwrapping what is unknown and new. Newlyweds Lauren and Christian are enjoying their honeymoon in Mexico (that's warm), and the Papanias welcomed their newest little one on December 31st. All wonderful gifts of love, consideration, and life that are given to us.

At the doctor's office yesterday, they gave me the "new patient" kit from the pharmaceutical company that makes my new IV chemotherapy drug. One of the main side effects of Doxil is a severe rash on feet and hands. Blisters and peeling skin, like a bad sunburn, often occur. It's recommended that I avoid friction and heat whenever possible. I should take tepid showers or baths, avoid holding coffee cups, doing dishes, and taking the warm clothes out of the dryer. (hmm, I'll miss the coffee cup warmth, but the others....)

The kit includes gel packs and cloths that I should freeze the packs and take to chemo. I will wrap the ice packs around my feet and hands during the treatment session. Dr. Koon said that they used to have patient keep their feet and hands in buckets of ice water during their infusions, but the gel packs are more tolerable. The idea is that the cold will constrict the blood vessels in those areas and less of the medication will reach those extremities.

I think I was doing okay until I went through the kit last night. The other common side effect is mouth sores. I had them for a while last time, and they're awful. I've been spending a lot of my time preparing myself for the emotional issues that accompany recurrence, but I haven't quite gotten a handle on the physical demand of these treatment rounds. I think it's the fear of not quite knowing what's beneath the wrapping that is upsetting me today.

Sarah Merdian

I know we've all read the words about courage and faith enabling us to go on despite fear, and I'm sure that I'll find that before next Monday. I have no doubt that the Baylor infusion nurses will be able to help me wrap up my hands and feet and by their grace and patience I will be able to feel comfort and maintain my dignity. I'm grateful that someone, somewhere has thought to use a soil fungus (the source of Doxil) to fight ovarian cancer. It has good results in many women.

I appreciate Dr. Koon telling me how lucky I am to have Dr. Coleman because "he knows more about chemotherapy than 90% of the physicians in our field. He travels and lectures all over the country. I'll learn from him." There's a possibility of another clinical trial in Houston later depending on my response to Doxil. Dr. Coleman listed many chemo options that are available from me. He is the best.

So this isn't how I envisioned 2008 getting under way, but that's how it goes. No new resolutions from me on this New Year's Day. I already feel like I'm on the right course. I'm just working on keeping a steady hand at the wheel.

Every blessing to each of you as your new year is unwrapped. I hope 2008 holds all that you treasure and all that you need. I pray that our year is filled with life, laughter, and loads of little miracles. Now, go eat some black-eyed peas (and my Aunt Linda will tell you to eat cabbage, too. It's for money in the new year.)

Yours 'til the auld lang synes,

Sarah

—◦—

January 03, 2008—10:29pm

The wonderful Megan, Dr. Koon's nurse, gave me a binder that Baylor is now providing for all cancer patients. It's informative and well-organized, and it even includes a glossary of terms. I think that there should also be a patient translation of MEDSPEAK phrases. Now, we know that I love my doctors, and I don't mean to generalize, but I'm noticing a pattern.

When you hear "There might be discomfort," it really means "This will hurt."

"You'll feel some pressure" = "You don't really want to know exactly what I'm doing"

"This may sting a little" = "This will hurt"

"Some people experience side effects" = "You WILL have side effects and one will likely be diarrhea."

"Take a deep breath"= "This will hurt"

"What flavor would you like?" = "This tastes so horrible that you'll probably shudder the next time you even hear the flavor's name spoken."

"I have a student working with me today" = "I'll be examining your body with someone who has not reached voting age."

and one of my personal favorites..........

"Here's a gown" = "Your modesty will be covered in the same way a postage stamp covers a bowling ball."

Yes, I'm learning to translate.

On a more serious note, I got some help today, and I can understand that all the unknowns are running wild in my imagination and making me feel scared. I don't know how much physical pain I'm going to experience—especially with the hands and feet thing, I've been feeling so good lately; it's hard to comprehend that I will feel worse in just a few days. I know that I'll get through it, but I'm just dreading walking into the infusion room.

I need to remember that life is a constant state of not knowing for certain what is coming next. Think of how many joyous surprises I would have missed if it were any other way. I can certainly make the most of my next few days. I go for acupuncture tomorrow, and I'm asking for the joy needles again. Take it where you find it.

Yours 'til the dread locks,

Sarah

PS—A picture from the wedding reception. What a grand time. Check it (and more photos) out on the SarahMerdian site at www.CarePages.com)

⁓

Jan. 06, 2008—5:50pm

I went to a wonderful dinner party last night that included a little fun word play. In that spirit, I offer the following quiz for the wordly wise.

1. Asthenia
   a. A Greek goddess
   b. A city in Georgia
   c. A loss of strength
   d. A torture for a lisper
2. Liposome
   a. Austrian horse breed
   b. Fat bubble
   c. Element used in batteries
   d. Spanish for "kiss me"
3. Palmar
   a. Pertaining to the hand
   b. Handwriting method
   c. Island near Belize
   d. You're soaking in it
4. Extravasation
   a. One more week off work
   b. To remove surgically
   c. Leakage of fluid out of its container
   d. Title of Liberace's last world tour
5. Bag balm
   a. Lotion designed for bovines

  b. Designer purse

  c. IV solution residue

  d. Derogatory golfing term

6. Berkus

  a. Peeling skin

  b. German footwear brand

  c. Oprah's designer

  d. Cucumber variety

7. Neutropenia

  a. Skin cleanser brand

  b. Small rodents found in Louisiana

  c. Result of Viagra overdose

  d. Low white blood cell count

8. LMD

  a. Love Me Do (Beatles' song)

  b. Lifetime Maximum Dose

  c. Least Multiple Divisor

  d. Local Mild Dyspepsia

As you can probably tell, I've been reading my Doxil info, and this is my calm before the storm. I'm doing okay. I'm a little less fearful, a little more hopeful, and a lot more ready just to get it going. I know I haven't returned all the phone calls and emails. I appreciate your patience.

Yours 'til the quiz bowls,

Sarah

Answers

 1.C 2.B 3.A 4.C 5.A 6.C 7.D 8.A

Ratings

 0 to 3 correct Nurse's aide

4 to 6 correct Lab tech

7 to 8 correct You watch Oprah?

~·~

January 07, 2008—7:24pm

When I suggested that the Doxil looked like Koolaid Khemo in either cherry or fruit punch, my sister replied, "So what are they trying to do? Ruin ALL the Jolly Rancher flavors?"

I've made it through my first round. It took twice as long as I expected, but I appreciate that Pam did a slow iv to make sure that I didn't have a reaction to the drug. She got the needle in on the second stick, and gave me a Tweety bird Bandaid for the first attempt hole.

I'm feeling tired and antsy and headachey and a little nauseous. I can scarcely believe that I had to turn the a/c on. Charles got me all set and I'm probably heading to bed before 8:00.

Pam did mention that tea tree oil would help keep my fingernails from falling off. I hadn't heard about that side effect. I swear, the fun never stops.

I did see James, a chemo nursing aide, who had offered to braid my hair last summer (I was bald at the time.) I reminded him about his offer and today he said, "Your hair is so wavy, it's making me seasick." Feeling the love.

Yours 'til the next wave (hopefully not of nausea),

Sarah

~·~

January 8, 2008

refresher from Dr. Michael Bedford

> **Cancer is so limited...it cannot cripple love, it**
> **cannot shatter hope, it cannot corrode faith,**

it cannot eat away peace, it cannot destroy
confidence, it cannot kill friendship, it cannot shut
out memories, it cannot silence courage, it cannot
invade the soul, it cannot reduce eternal life, it
cannot quench the Spirit, it cannot lessen the
power of the Resurrection.

January 09, 2008—6:11pm

My postal carrier is a peach of a guy. He takes the time to leave my packages on my back steps if I'm not home. He has observed my transformation throughout treatment and always takes the time to ask how I'm doing and has added me to his prayer list. He shared his mother's diagnosis of cancer last fall, and I just learned that his absence during the last part of December was due to her death. She just couldn't handle the chemo. Still he is concerned about me. Today he brought me three things: prescription refills, the newest issue of CURE (Cancer Updates, Research & Education) magazine and a card from a family member. How delightful—something for my body, mind, and soul.

This CURE issue has an article on ovarian cancer and wouldn't you know it, but in the NEW APPROACHES section of the article, my own Dr. Coleman is quoted. He says, "Our challenge is to determine which drug goes with which patient and which cocktail would be appropriate." Sounds just like my guy. Sounds like he's talking about me.

I'm at day 3 of this new chemo cycle, and I'm doing really well. My headache is gone, and now I'm just battling some light nausea and fatigue. I'm doing all the precautionary measures for the Hand-Foot Syndrome and mouth sores. So far, so good. I even went swimming today, and I'm heading into school tomorrow.

I spoke to Megan (Dr. Koon's nurse) today about my concern regarding my latest CA-125 results. My number had gone up from a 16 in September to a 30 on December 21st at MDA. My Baylor CA-125 blood test, taken on December 31st, came back at 75. This is quite a jump.

This issue of CURE magazine states that "Physicians who specialize in ovarian cancer often have a love-hate relationship with CA-125." It's good for reporting recurrence AND should be taken in consideration of other factors as well (such as my CT scan). Each report that I've ever gotten from Baylor has a disclaimer about comparing the tests from different manufacturers. Megan says that could be a reason for a discrepancy. She also stated that even if we are comparing apples to apples and the test is accurate, it indicates that we're doing the right thing by starting this chemo. I have looked online and found that some women have CA-125 reports in the 300s. I've never had one above 77 (last February).

There have been many times during this cancer journey when a "number" has been alarming to me at first. I need to remember that such measurements are abstract, and my body doesn't know stage IV or 2.5 cm or even CA-125. I asked Dr. Coleman for some numbers (or odds or percentages), and as far as he was concerned, my number was either a zero or a one. The treatment will fit me or it will not. If it doesn't fit, we'd go on to something else.

When he examined my incision progress last month (now a 48" scar rather than an incision), Dr. Coleman told me, "You're the best healer ever." I feel the same way about him. I feel I'm on the right course.

Yours 'til the next issue,

Sarah

January 11, 2008—9:53am

Hold a true friend with both your hands.
—Nigerian Proverb

So Charles picks me up from chemo on Monday and takes me to Whole Foods so I can get some ginger ale because I'm so nauseous. He takes me home, pours my glass, gets me settled and even holds my hand as I cry. This whole thing can just be overwhelming. He waits until I'm okay, and then he heads home.

About thirty minutes later, Charles calls me with a question. He wants to know if I think the raw chicken that has been in the fridge for about a week will still be good. I can't believe this. He has called the ONE PERSON ON THE PLANET that he knows for certain is nauseous, and has asked about rotten raw chicken. God love that guy. I certainly do.

I simply can't imagine getting through the past year without Charles. I can't imagine living the past 29 years without him either. He's always there with what I need even when I am not sure myself. Charles has shared in my brightest days and my darkest hours with strength, acceptance, patience, and love. I am a better person because of him.

Today is Charles' birthday, and I wish him every happiness and every blessing, and I look forward to our next adventure.

Yours 'til he takes the cake,

Sarah

PS—You know, I love Charles so much, that I'm scarcely bothered (any more) when my neighbor refers to him as my son, or my Aunt Frances calls him to get my number and then forgets to call me, or when the Thai restaurant employees see me and ask, "Where is Charles?"

January 13, 2008—9:23pm
Elisabeth Kubler-Ross, a psychiatrist who wrote *On Death and Dying* in the late sixties, describes the process by which we handle

loss and tragedy (or the diagnosis of a terminal illness) as the five stages of grief.

Denial
Anger
Bargaining
Depression
Acceptance

Here's what I've noticed:

- The steps are not necessarily sequential, and there seems to be an ebb and flow. Imagine a wave of sadness or anger and then the next wave-acceptance-washes over and the anger recedes with the undertow. The next wave may still be acceptance, or maybe fear, or peace, or joy. Each existing as a current that is both independent and part of the whole.
- The people around you, the people who love you, experience the same stages, and are often at a different place...........and that is okay.
- Talking about death is hard for most everyone. Funny thing is that it's not just about cancer and me ....we're all headed in that direction eventually. Let's not make it scarier or lonelier than it needs to be. I was able to talk to someone and really explore some of the fear I was feeling about my chemo and side effects and expectations. That very process made it easier for me to handle.
- Sometimes people view acceptance as giving up. I love this quote:

Acceptance is not submission; it is acknowledgement
of the facts of a situation. Then deciding what
you're going to do about it.
                    —Kathleen Casey Theisen

Here are the facts of my situation: If this chemo works, then I will probably stay on it. Dr. Koon says he has a patient who has been on Doxil for 24 months, and it's keeping her cancer at bay. If it doesn't work, then I'll go on another type of chemo.

Here's what I'm working to accept: My cancer is likely a chronic condition and treatment will probably be part of the rest of my life. Maybe monthly, maybe weekly, maybe something in between. A lady at Gilda's Club once told me, "I'm just working on staying alive long enough for them to find the cure." I can accept that.

I've had a quite an amount of information and experience to absorb in the past couple weeks. I don't always go forward, but I end up ahead. I don't always feel strong, but I do find strength. I don't mean to dwell, but sometimes it feels that the water is up to my ankles and rising......sometimes. Luckily, on most days, my spirits, among other things, remain quite buoyant.

Yours 'til the root beer floats,

Sarah

January 19, 2008—11:05

Laughter and tears are both responses to frustra-
tion and exhaustion . . . . I myself prefer to laugh,
since there is less cleaning up to do afterward.
                    —Kurt Vonnegut, Jr.

Perhaps we shared in a few of these frustrations this week:

- traffic
- car problems
- running toilet
- that smell in the fridge
- technology roadblocks
- recycling overflow
- cabinet space
- work
- installing a new printer
- the insurance premium
- there's nothing for dinner
- no nap time

Let me tell you, I look back on my week, and I'm delighted that these have been my frustrations. How wonderful that I'm not worrying about cancer, or nagging abdominal pain (turns out that's another side effect of Doxil), or nausea, or life and death. I am not trying to trivialize any of these situations, it's just nice that the veil has been lifted on a little bit of perspective.

PH, you're right. We can do anything for at least a little while. We can handle what comes, and we don't have to do it alone.

This busy workweek has left me tired (like already in my nightgown in bed by 5:00 tired), but I'm feeling so much better than my chemo week. I go in Monday for blood labs. They'll tell me how my infection fighters are doing and if I need to alter activities as a result.

I enjoyed seeing so many kids and families at Peak carpool yesterday. Despite the cold, it gave me such a warm feeling. It's nice to feel like a part of something. Enjoy the long weekend and stay warm.

Yours 'til the next weak,

Sarah

January 21, 2008—4:58pm

> *I wonder if illiterate people get the full effect of*
> *alphabet soup?* —**Jerry Seinfeld**

Certainly during the past year, my favorite letter of the alphabet has been the big C. Very little trumps the C card, and I use that just about every time I can. So imagine my LOL when I got to Baylor for blood work today and noticed that someone has taken the big C right off the cancer building. Sure, it's possible that the letter fell off, but I'm hoping that someone took it and I'm hoping that they give it to ME! I'm not a rap star, so I won't wear it on a chain (Sorry Flavor Flav), but I sure would hang it up in my house; maybe on my front door.

Also, the irony of the place being the phonetic "answer" center is not lost on me. I got an answer that I wanted today. I asked Megan, my favorite nurse, if I could have "the occasional glass of red wine." I've been Googling "Doxil" and "alcohol" and have had no luck. (Is it my inner 5th grader who keeps asking until the right answer is given?) Cheers it is.

Last week at my support group, where we always discuss the most urgent of issues, I suggested that stores start offering a cancer registry (you know, like a wedding or baby registry). Needless to say, it's just ten more days until my first cancer-versary. Considering the dire nature of this disease, the traditional anniversary listing certainly must be bumped up a little from the wedding fare. Anyone who has dealt with any health care issues for a year certainly needs no more PAPER. I'll get back to you when I get more info on this topic. Or at least the answer I want. I'm just saying.

Yours 'til it's letter perfect,

Sarah

Sarah Merdian

January 27, 2008—10:13am

> *Fatigue is the best pillow.*   —Benjamin Franklin

Turns out many people get alarmed when I mention that I'm sorta looking forward to my chemo just so I can get some rest. Well, it's true.

My past couple weeks of working in schools have been exhausting for me. I find myself in bed before dark not necessarily going to sleep, but I'm too tired to stay up. Since the stealthy Doxil circulates in the blood for an extended period of time, I shouldn't be surprised with this fatigue.

My skin has been dry (hello winter) and my feet are starting to have some of the unpleasant side effects. For all of us who remember the Dr. Scholl's wooden sole sandals of the 1970s, think of the slide-back-heel-bruise all over the bottom of your feet. The good news is that it only hurts when I stand or walk. I got some good tips from one of my support group members.

I'm also finding that I'm having a little hair loss. Hard to believe that hair loss was SUCH A BIG DEAL to me six months ago. Today, I'm scarcely fazed. There's something to be said about cancer and perspective and self-acceptance. So, if we're summing up:

Sick
Tired
Flaky
Sore
Slightly shedding
Looks forward to chemo

Yep, I think I'm ready to go work on my eHarmony.com profile. Yours 'til I'm the sole survivor,

Sarah

January 31, 2008—10:05am

A year ago, I had a belly button.

A year ago today, my ob/gyn told me that I had cancer. After our discussion while the nurse set up the oncology appointment, the doctor mentioned, "You know, when your pathology report came in yesterday afternoon, I said, "This is SO lucky!" because it reminded me that today's the last day to get my son's application turned in to your school." It's a year later, and you can call me Lady Luck on my first cancer-versary.(And that's not just because my sister swears that wearing my INF pin or cancer bracelet ALWAYS makes her win at the casino. Really glad I can help.)

Here I am today trying to get through a coughy, chesty, raspy, lousy feeling day so I can hop into chemo on Monday. (I know there's a little of the alcohol swab for the lethal injection logic working there.)

To say it's been a rollercoaster ride is probably an understatement. It's certainly been a journey. Sometimes I've taken my own steps and other times I've been carried (or rolled or pulled along). Sometimes I've stumbled, but most of the time I've been guided along the right path. Many times I've been able just to stand still and appreciate the view.

I think I've been able to laugh every day during the past year. (maybe not the icu day, but I've certainly made up for it the next day when I had to hold my incision while I laughed so hard at my custom message from Antonio Banderas you might still be able to view that video at http://207.56.113.230/sarah/index.html).

I read that "An anniversary is a time to celebrate the joys of today, the memories of yesterday, and the hopes of tomorrow." Sounds exactly perfect for me today.

So when I blow on the candle on my anniversary cake (Charles, I'm getting a cake, right?) I'll make the following wish. (It's okay to say anniversary wishes out loud. Check the birthday handbook for details.)

Sarah Merdian

I wish that we all receive—

- The strength we need to carry through,
- The wisdom to know what we're meant to do,
- Patience for others and ourselves each day.
- And faith to guide us along the way.

Yours 'til the belly buttons and the lucky strikes,

Sarah

—❦—

February 04, 2008—06:11pm

> *Adversity is the diamond dust Heaven polishes its jewels with.*   —**Thomas Carlyle**

It's the collection of treasured moments that make our lives sparkle and shine, and like a geode, one never quite knows what setting holds the next jewel.

Such is Sophia Grace and her cute smile (in the darling outfit that her Aunt Sarah sent her). What a sweetie. I am so touched that Mark and Karen have asked me to be Sophia Grace's godmother. It's such an honor to be asked, especially when I know that I am often unsteady in spirit.

I felt that I owed it to Mark and Karen to offer an out, and maybe they wanted to ask someone else who has a better chance at being around longer. (I am now referring to this as my "shelf life." I'm not trying to be morose or pessimistic, but it is part of my reality. However, as our friend John A. will tell you, those dates stamped on products are not really "expiration" dates.........they're "best by" dates. Certainly the BEST is yet to come.)

Yet, Karen and Mark are willing to take me as long as I last, and I'm grateful. The baptism is on Easter Sunday, and I hope,

hope, hope that I'll be able to travel to Atlanta to be there for the big day.

Today in the blood lab waiting room, two Italian greyhounds were making the rounds as part of Baylor's pet therapy program. It's really amazing to see how some patients light up at their presence. How funny that the dogs' names were Sophie and Gracie, and they came right over and hopped into my lap.

Kristina, my chemo nurse, got my iv going with a near painless stick (yippee), and things went smoothly. My session was less than two hours today. I'm home and tired with a bit of a headache and a slightly queasy stomach.

Almost every chemo patient deals with nausea at various times. Imagine my surprise to see the patient next to me having SUSHI for lunch. I mean, ICK! You'd think there would be some sort of Chemo Code of Conduct:

> No gorgonzola
> No rotten chicken
> No dog farts
> No sushi

I'm just saying.

As a side note, I feel that I should mention that my 20 generic anti-nausea pills had a co-pay of $10 today, but the total price was $718.25. Today's dose of semi-precious ruby red Doxil has a list price of $8272.00. My portion is a mere fraction. I'm definitely not endorsing any platform, but it seems imperative that we should know where our candidates stand on health care. It's a tough topic with many facets and no easy solution. (We certainly don't need to make my CarePage the forum for that discussion. YIKES!) It's just something to think about. I know I need to do some research and reflection.

So another chemo is history, and I have the next few days to recharge and recuperate. I thank everyone for the endless support, messages, thoughts, and prayers. As the Mastercard folks would say, priceless.

Yours 'til the bling blings,

Sarah

PS—Yes, Thomas Carlyle should have known better than to end his quote with a preposition. You know the old saying— Copy-and-pasters can't be choosers.

———

February 07, 2008—10:51am

Comfort comes with knowing.

After my first cycle of Doxil, I experienced somewhat severe abdominal pain. Of course my imagination took off, and all I could envision was my cancer exploding and expanding. Maybe I was feeling the Doxil brigade on a full frontal attack in the Battle of the Lymph Node (feel free to whistle the Bridge over the River Kwai theme here). Maybe I had pulled a muscle (again) by lifting the cases of Costco bottled water. It was painful and scary. Today, the same physical sensation is present, but this time I know that abdominal pain is a side effect of Doxil. It's certainly easier to deal with the concerns of "what is" rather than the phantoms of "what-could-it-be."

Monday night found me vomiting and sleepless. I've experienced a fatigue and weariness all week. I did catch up a little on Tuesday night with 9 blissful hours of sleep and a 1.5 hour nap on Wednesday. Last night was more restless, but my stomach is more settled. Two steps forward, one step back.

Recuperation is seldom a linear progression, but rather an up and down collection of experiences filled with multiple tangents, frequent setbacks, and few shortcuts. But really, all of our human processes recovery, change, acceptance, understanding, faith, and forgiveness follow the same transitional path. Here the comfort might just be knowing that we're moving in the right direction even if the progress is slower or more uneven than we hoped.

I'm appreciative of the support I've received from my job. I feel like I can take the time I need to feel better. I'm warm and well-fed, and I enjoy reading everyone's posts and cards and emails. It's still hard for me to return all messages, but know that I appreciate hearing from you. I expect to be through this part of the ride in just a few days.

Yours 'til the merry-go-round,

Sarah

—~ ~—

February 09, 2008 —11:46am

> *That tingling sensation means it's working.*
> —Selsun Blue ad

I don't think the phrase is "What's good for the dander is good for the…deuce", but I've got two pair (elbows and knees) that are itching up a storm.

I've been expecting a rash on my hands and feet, but there's never a dull moment in chemo, and my arms and legs are currently hosting the seasonally appropriate Valentine redness. Of course it itches like crazy. I've got some prescription ointment that's helping a little bit. I'll check in with the nurse on Monday.

So the nausea's gone and the abdominal pain is nearly a memory, and I'm hoping that the cancer's getting just as irritated as my skin. I know the Doxil is a new approach for my cancer, but this gives whole new meaning to "starting from scratch."

I'm hanging in there.

Yours 'til the rash decisions,

Sarah

—~ ~—

  Sarah Merdian

February 14, 2008—2:20pm

During my last teaching year in Kansas, parents organized a Valentine's Day party complete with games. One activity was called FAMOUS PAIRS. Each student had a name written on a paper heart taped to his/her back and they were challenged to find their other half or mate. Of course we had Mickey and Minnie Mouse, Lilo and Stitch, Lady and the Tramp, Daisy and Donald Duck and Snow White and Prince Charming. It was chaotic, and the kids had fun.

Most kids took their paper hearts off after the games, but a few liked wearing them. Unfortunately, one mother arrived a little late and was OUTRAGED to see that her daughter was walking around the school with "The Tramp" written on her back. Sometimes, the context is everything.

This morning I sat in a school front office as students rushed in with arms full of glittered Valentine's boxes, flowers, and party supplies. Even at 8:00am, the chocolate buzz filled the air.

Last Valentine's Day was such an emotional time for me. I'd just found out about the cancer and surgery, and I was continually yoyo-ing between classroom and doctors' offices. Valentine's Day with my students was a brief respite of normalcy for me.

Fifth graders always make my day. We enjoy the marriage of class objectives (graphing, measurement, sentence structure, and creative writing) and conversation hearts. Candy isn't eaten at school, but we share Valentines as expressions of humor, friendship, and caring. We say thank you and laugh. I stole an idea for a former colleague and staple all of my Valentines to my shirt and walk out to dismissal in full regalia. That's wearing your heart on your sleeve.

Working with groups of students today made me feel a little less disconnected from the experience. I know that 24 years of being able to "do what you love" has truly been a blessing for me. I wonder if I'll ever be up to returning to the classroom, and I must admit there's always a sense of loss a loss of self and purpose and contribution and control. It's always hard to be separated from your love, your passion especially on Valentine's Day.

I hope that each of you gets to enjoy all that you love today..........and everyday.

Yours 'til the work wonders,

Sarah

⁓

February 18, 2008—3:59pm

> *We are all special cases.*   **—Albert Camus**

Last week as I looked in the mirror at the back of my raised arm to check out the extent of the rash, I noticed a discolored patch of skin. The brown blotch is on my upper inner arm (you know, the flabbiest part) and at first I thought it was something that might just wash off. (Let me know as soon as I start oversharing, okay?)

Well, of course, it didn't wash off and that led the next logical conclusion melanoma. Certainly you get some sort of frequent flyer pass if you have THREE kinds of cancer, right?

Megan, my wonderful nurse, had told me to stop by after my blood labs today so she could look at the rash. I didn't have an official appointment, so she just came out to the waiting room where I proceeded to show her both the rash (it's clearing up somewhat) and the melanoma patch.

First of all, I'm glad that I've reached that non-modesty point which lets me partially undress in a doctor's waiting room, and apologies to the other patients that were present. My rash has Megan and Dr. Koon stumped. They're surprised that Benadryl didn't help. I feel so special.

Secondly, I'm thrilled that I don't have skin cancer. However it is a smidge disconcerting to hear that I have hand-foot syndrome…in my armpit. Friction causes the reaction. Good thing I was scrubbing it, eh? At least it doesn't hurt, or itch, or burn, or show.

I'm waiting to hear the blood test results. So far my numbers have been good. I'm noticing that these chemo cycles do not have the same upwardly mobile energy and stamina curve as my last rounds. I find that I'm not feeling any better as the time passes. Perhaps it's the nature of the slow release medication. It's taxing on my body and spirit. We'll see.

Yours 'til the pit stops,

Sarah

PS—A special thought goes to my nieces who lost their grandmother last week. Alice was a daily presence in her granddaughters' lives, and she will be missed. I have no doubt that she will continue to watch over them as they grow up.

February 25, 2008—5:21pm

Who smiles like the cutest angel and snorts like a littlest pig? It's baby Sophia straight from heaven (by way of the farm?)

What a thrill to see Karen and Sophia in Dallas this weekend. The baby is simply precious. It's incredible to see the love and affection that such a wee one can summon up in those around her. To say that her sisters dote on her is quite an understatement.

I wish I had just a fraction of Karen's stamina. She's patient, brave, and open all on just a few hours of sleep. She keeps her sense of humor, and she even brought homemade cookies for everyone!

I fly down to the Valley for a school visit tomorrow, and then I'll go to St. Louis on Saturday for a wedding. I'll get back in town just in time for chemo next Monday. I have 5 small trips planned for March. I guess I refuse to stand still to make sure that I'm still standing.

Yours 'til the baby's pampered,

Sarah

PS—March is mess formatting wise and I don't know how to fix
it! Where is a computer geek when I need one???

~

March 03, 2008—8:33pm

> **Peace is the deliberate adjustment of my life to the**
> **will of God.** **—Unknown**

Okay, it's safe to say that I'm not yet at peace. I'm trying, but I
haven't arrived.

The last ten days have been somewhat frenzied for me. Lovely
guests, rewarding travel, involved work, and shared celebrations have
all been wonderful, yet tremendously draining.

I think about how I currently feel. I'm able to "live" about 75% of
my "life." I can accept that trade off, but I wonder when do I say that
it's not a sufficient? 50%? 25%? How much is enough? I can't imagine
NOT grasping at even 1% if it included even some of the collected
treasured moments that I've experienced in the past few weeks.

I often hear that I should do whatever "I want to do." If I want to
rest, or go to a function later, or leave early, or skip something all
together because I'm tired, people are very patient, and understanding
and supportive. However, I don't think they understand that I'm not
choosing something that I "want" at all. It's exactly what I don't
want. I don't want to miss out or lie in bed or let life pass me by. I
feel more MUSTS than WANTS at those times.

Today I asked Dr. Koon about my current level of fatigue. I
mentioned that with my previous chemo, I suffered more side effects
early, but then I noticed an upswing of energy and stamina. I'm not
seeing that surge these days.

Doxil does not hit me as hard as last summer's rounds, so he believes that there is not the discrepancy (and thereby ensuing increase) in my energy levels. I guess that makes sense, but I admit that it is somewhat discouraging to make peace with the reality that this is my very best. If my March 25th scan shows that the Doxil is working, I'll continue on it. That means I'll probably continue to feel this way.....including the rash. The rash.

The rash.

The rash comes from friction. Capillaries break, and the Doxil irritates the tissue under the skin. The rash is spreading in a barber pole pattern up my arms, and also on the inner part of my knees. It's bumpy and itchy and bright red. It's irritating.....in so many ways. I even find myself missing the physical and mental benefits of swimming, but I can't imagine anyone letting Suzy Speckled into the pool.

Right now Dr. Koon wants to see if he can make me more comfortable. (I'm all FOR that.) He thinks that he remembers a study in which steroids lessen these side effects. (In fact, he thinks that Dr. Coleman even participated in that study. What's not to love about this guy?). I'll find out later this week. I know that I'll probably be ruining my major league baseball eligibility, however…

So chemo went okay today. My CA-125 (the tumor marker blood test) is starting to decline (that's good news!), and I have everything I need to get through the next few days. It's probably a few days where I'll be prone to do my usual over-thinking, but I seem to need the process to work through my struggles.

On a lighter note if a reference to an obituary about an untimely death can be considered "lighter" I did have to laugh out loud on the plane to St. Louis. I was looking through the Dallas paper and stumbled upon the obituaries. I don't often read the paper, but sometimes I have to look at the obituaries and see if any younger people have died and if it was due to cancer. I know it's morbid in a way, but it makes me feel that such a reality can be faced. It's sort of a shared sadness/shared strength thing. Anyway, I was surprised to read of the death of a man who was born in 1964. I was more surprised to discover that his nickname was "Lucky." All blessings to him. Living or not, may we all be at peace.

Yours 'til the percent ages,

Sarah

———❦———

March 09, 2008—9:54am

> *When late morning rolls around and you're feeling*
> *a bit out of sorts, don't worry; you're probably just*
> *a little eleven o'clockish.*
> **—Winnie-the-Pooh**

Well, I'm not going to just blame the time change. Dr. Koon's office got the steroids to me last week. They are helping the rash. The itching, spreading, and sensitivity have decreased significantly. The bumps are still visible, but lessening.

Of course, as Roseanne Roseannadanna (our dear Gilda Radner) would say, "It's always something." Yes the rash is being treated, but here comes the side effects of the 6-day steroid treatment: horrible acid reflux and nausea, jitters, sleeplessness, and mood swings.

I'll finish these pills up soon, and then we'll see what happens next. (I feel like that is my mantra. Wait and see. Wait and see. Try not to over think and wait and see. Attempt some sort of normalcy as you wait, wait, wait. Keep a positive attitude and wait. Occupy your mind with other things and wait. Try not to feel helpless and that things are completely out of your control, and be patient, and wait and see. Wait, and then find out more, and then do more, and then wait and see.)

However, I do have many high points as well. After this chemo week, I am finally feeling somewhat recharged. I'm ready to head back to schools next week and then on to NYC next weekend. I enjoyed a lovely evening at Lake Kiowa on Friday, and I just finished reading the wonderful children's book *Project Mulberry* in hopes of meeting the author later this month in KC. AND, I'm in love with Starbuck's new honey latte. Simple pleasures in a complicated time.

Yours 'til spring forwards,

Sarah

PS—I was part of a one-on-one research study for CarePages last week. The staff had been interviewing people around the country and was most impressed with the 23,000+ visits to this page. They hadn't encountered anything quite like that previously. My point of my interview was the connection provided by the use of their site. Continuing thanks for all of your support.

———

March 13, 2008—4:09pm
Sometimes, we don't know JACK.

I have the body that's fighting back.

This is the cancer
That invades the body that's fighting back.

This is the chemo
That gives cancer a whack
That invades the body that's fighting back.

This is the rash
That comes from the chemo
That gives cancer a whack
That invades the body that's fighting back.

This is the steroid
That calms the rash
That comes from chemo
that cancer whack,
That invades the body that's fighting back

This is the reflux
That bubbles from steroids
That calms the rash
That comes from chemo
That gives cancer a whack
That invades the body that's fighting back

This is the sore throat
After the reflux
That steroid influx
To limit the itch
The Doxil blood which
Gives cancer a whack
That invades the body that's fighting back

This is the insomnia
that comes from the pill
For the sore throat
That comes windblown still
After the reflux
That calms the rash
That comes from chemo
That gives cancer a whack
That invades the body that's fighting back

This is the body that starts to shake
The lower lip that starts to quake

  Sarah Merdian

From the insomnia
That comes from the pill
For the sore throat
and the gathering sneeze
After the reflux
Of the steroid breeze
That calms the rash
From the chemo crash
That gives cancer a whack
That invades the body that's fighting back

This is me.
Often feeling discouraged
Trying to find courage
In the quake
And the shake
In the wide wide awake
Propping up straight
Sitting up late
From the endless pills
The teardrop spills
The reflux burns
The stomach turns
The bumpy rash
The chemo stash
That I request
Come be my guest
In my body that's fighting back.

This
is
me
today.

Yours 'til the nursery rhymes,

Sarah

—◦◦—

March 17, 2008—02:07am

The Mystery by Van Morrison

Let go into the mystery
Let yourself go
And when you open up your heart
You get everything you need
Baby there's a way and a mystic road
You've got to have some faith
To carry on[5]

As I was sitting at the Van Morrison concert on Saturday, I couldn't help thinking about whether or not I was "crossing something off my bucket list." How could I enjoy being in that very moment AND realize by its very nature, that such a moment was fleeting, and finite, and limited. The idea of "doing this one thing" before you die means that after you do it....you're that much closer to being gone. It's a mixed bag of emotions for me.

We had heard from a few sources that Van's show would probably only be about an hour and would focus primarily on his new CD coming out in April. Still, I gave myself permission to enjoy whatever came and hope for the best a few old classics, and hey, maybe even the Chieftains (who are playing in NYC on Monday) would be kind enough to stop on by.

It's a long journey not only to New York City, but up to 175 Street and Broadway where the "Byzantine—Romanesque—Indo—Hindu—Sino—Moorish—Persian—Eclectic—Rococo—Deco" style

United Palace has stood since the 1930s. Reverend Ike has church services there each week and you're asked to "Come on in or pass with a smile." Today, a Dominican neighborhood surrounds the Palace, and I enjoyed a glimpse of a New York that was new to me.

It's hard for me nearly impossible to separate my physical struggles with the daily goings on of my life. My back and rash hurt during my entire trip. My stomach revolts at inopportune moments, and my fatigue and self-composure hang from Damocles' thread. Yet, I wedged my butt into my last row on the floor seat and got to enjoy the show.

Van Morrison and his band were right on the money. Tight. Sharp. Bold. Seamless. Fine tuned. He did play a few oldies (not the big classics) and then several new songs. I loved each and every song. He never really spoke to the audience, but it was evident that he was putting every bit of himself into the music. The show ran a little over 90 minutes with no encore, no Chieftains, no guru, no method, no teacher. I'll definitely be purchasing "Keep It Simple" on April 1st.

Somewhere during the concert, I made a switch. I realized that I wasn't just checking something off my list before I died. I found myself wondering about what my next Van Morrison concert would be like. It's a strange sensation going from "I'm living my life" approach to the "I'm not finished living my life" perspective. I thought—wow, what a great idea the INF tattoo turned out to be. It's exactly right. Daring to risk was leading me to the place where I could dare to dream and hope and wonder.

Now, this apparent calm and self-awareness is what it is, and it didn't really help me 10 minutes after the concert when I hit the emotional wall of fatigue and physical discomfort combined with transportation uncertainties. I found myself sobbing and overwhelmed and in pain and questioning this whole plan in general. However, Team Merd came through as always (even though Charles did tell me not to lean up against him and get crybaby mascara on his coat), and dear Bill, Steph, Charles, and Michael had me shuttled back to my cozy bed in no time.

So I'm back home. Totally exhausted, yet better for the journey.

It's St. Patrick's Day, so here's an Irish blessing for us all: May the Good Lord take a liking to you... but not too soon!

Yours 'til concert halls,

Sarah

March 27, 2008—7:49am

> *I am not discouraged, because every wrong*
> *attempt discarded is another step forward.*
> **—Thomas A. Edison**

I wish I had the patience of Edison then maybe I could also feel NOT discouraged, but I do. I'm disappointed with the Doxil results, frustrated that 3 months of fatigue and itching might have been for naught, and concerned that I'm not up to the challenge of the next step. However, I do agree that every failed attempt is just a step along the way to the best thing. Anne Morrow Lindbergh said, "It takes as much courage to have tried and failed as it does to have tried and succeeded."

When Dr. Coleman suggested the Erbitux trial, I realized that I had left our December meeting with a negative impression of that clinical trial. I had the idea that it wasn't being successful, so why would I want to try it? The best part of talking to Dr. Coleman is his openness and ability to listen and respond. He wanted to know what I was feeling and he didn't want me to do anything that I was uncomfortable doing. He explained that Erbitux (which is primarily a colorectal cancer recurrence drug, but it is being tested in ovarian cancer recurrence) IS working for some patients and is not working for others. He doesn't want to miss an opportunity for me, and we'd try it for a couple months and then reassess.

I think every Uplift classroom has an action wheel posted in the room. The three components, linked by arrows, read: Act '! Reflect '! Choose. It's a cycle that repeats, just like every step of this process has been. Right now, Dr. Coleman (and his fellow Dr. Kamat) are presenting my case to their team. He wants input from the radiologists as well as other colleagues regarding my case. Radiation is a possibility. Other chemotherapy is a possibility. We shall see.

(and poor Dan yesterday he MEANT to say, "They're not doing a BIOPSY right now" but what he actually said was, "They're not doing an AUTOPSY right now." Yes, a biopsy is also a possibility. I'm hoping to hold off the autopsy for quite a while.)

So, going back to Thomas A. Edison, the light bulb is a good reference point for the tumors (which I'm calling the WATT brothers We're a Tumor Trio). The biggest Watt brother is about the size of an outdoor house Christmas bulb, and the smaller ones are a little bigger than an indoor Christmas tree light. I don't think they're flashing different colors, but I'm betting they're all a shade of red or pink. This image certainly begs the question "How many doctors/chemo sessions does it take to remove a light bulb?"

I did inquire about Erbitux's side effects. An "acne-like" rash tops the list. Good grief. Of course I appreciate your prayers for healing, but I also am in dire need of strength and patience. Tuesday was the longest day. I woke up in Atlanta at 4:30am, landed in Houston around 11:00am, and left M D Anderson around 7:30 pm. I got to do my blue wall pictures for Dr. Butler, blood tests, x-rays and then the CT scan. Seeing Dr. Coleman the next morning certainly was the high point of the visit. I think we all were hoping for better news. However, I must remember that "we'll try something else" is far better than "there's nothing left to try." I'll hear today or tomorrow about the next effort.

Yours 'til the light switches,

Sarah

March 29, 2008—8:22am

I'm not a fan of reality TV. The shows are painfully drawn out and slow moving. The performance shows with the "let's axe a person this week" format are not entertaining for me, and I cannot stomach when the self proclaimed "expert" lowers the boom or lifts the spirit of the contestants as if someone else's opinion is what matters most.

This past weekend, I heard a lot of talk about "What Not to Wear." I'd never seen the show, and we all laughed about the ancient clothing that hangs in each of our own closets. Yesterday, when I was mind-numbingly surfing through the channels, I happened upon WNTW, and thought I've give it a chance.

Well, the subject of this segment was a former exotic dancer who currently wears outfits that are QUITE revealing and......I can't make this up.....likes to make a good first impression and express her individuality by wearing a raccoon tail attached to her jeans, skirts, whatever. Her skanky outfits are preventing her and her fiancé from getting into the nicer clubs (clearly, a negative effect on their lives), and the experts think the tail MIGHT BE SENDING THE WRONG MESSAGE. In the flash forward before the commercial break, we see the poor thing, sobbing uncontrollably and saying, "When they took it, it felt like they were taking a part of me."

That's five minutes of my life that I'm never getting back.

I heard from MDA yesterday. Dr. Han (who had been on my hospital team a year ago) called to share the consensus from the interdisciplinary team meeting. Since my tumors have different locations, radiation is not an option for me. They do suggest chemotherapy treatment as the next step, and she listed three chemo options: Taxotere, Topotecan, and Taxol all done weekly.

I asked her about the Erbitux clinical trial at MDA. Dr. Coleman had noted that I was not interested in participating in this trial, so it was not discussed with the team. I had expressed my negative feelings about the trial, and he had taken my feelings to heart in planning for my treatment.

Of course, since Wednesday, I've had a change of heart about participating in the trial. I know that my attitude toward the topic was based on the idea that the Erbitux was NOT showing much benefit for the patients involved in the study. Dr. Coleman explained that like every other cancer drug it works for some people and it doesn't work for others. This respect.....inclusion....focus of the individual patient in cancer treatment is something I love about Dr. Coleman. The Erbitux trial could be a great opportunity even though it would mean traveling to Houston once a week for treatment.

If Dr. Coleman could only be my expert, and take out the Watt Brothers in the way Stacy London would snatch a Delta Burke/ Suzanne Sugarbaker ruffle-at-the-waist dress (or raccoon tail) from anyone's closet, I'd happily let him. However, all he can/will do is offer suggestions, guidance, and his best opinions. The decision is really up to me. Knowing that he considered my wishes and comfort level at the team presentation means the world to me.

Dr. Coleman is out of Houston for the next couple weeks, but Dr. Han is going to email him. She'll let him know that I am open to the clinical trial and get more details on that option. Dr. Han will let me know what Dr. Coleman thinks, and we'll go from there.

> My reality is that I get to wait and hear.
> Deal or No Deal.
> The Amazing Race.
> The Real World.
> Survivor.

Yours 'til the tail spins,

Sarah

April 02, 2008—8:50am

> *The waiting is the hardest part.*
> *Every day you see one more card*
> *You take it on faith, you take it to the heart*
> *The waiting is the hardest part.*
> —Tom Petty[6]

Mary just sent me a Dallas Morning News article where a cancer survivor states that "waiting is the worst side effect of cancer." I don't know if it's the worst, but I'd put it in my top 5 list.

I spoke to Liz, Dr. Coleman's assistant yesterday since I haven't heard back from Dr. Han. Liz explained that Dr. C was on his way to Germany. "He's going over there to learn about some new medicine, so that's exciting. " (We love Liz). He will return early next week to the US but is serving as an examiner for doctors taking their boards. He'll be back in the clinic on Wednesday.

There is still a possibility Dr. Han will get some email info from Dr. Coleman before his return, but I just trying to stay patient. The best news for me is that during this little respite from chemo, the rash is all but gone and I'm feeling more rested. I'm working some this week as well. It's good to have my mind occupied with meaningful matters.

So it's not a no news is good news situation. It simply means no news is no news. I'll keep you posted.

Yours 'til the wait lifts,

Sarah

April 03, 2008—10:15pm

rodent: *n. Any of various mammals of the order Rodentia, such as a mouse, rat, squirrel, or beaver, characterized by large incisors adapted for gnawing or nibbling.*

I'm going to be a guinea pig.

Today I spoke to Debbie, the research nurse at M. D. Anderson, and I'm scheduled to begin the Erbitux clinical trial next Wednesday. This is the study that Dr. Coleman recommended.

I'll go down to Houston weekly for the next two months. They'll monitor my blood levels each week, and I'll see Dr. Coleman again in a month. At the end of the two-month cycle, they'll do new scans and reassess.

Erbitux is currently approved for treatment with colorectal cancer. This study is investigating its use with endometrial cancers. From what I understand, the drug prevents cancer cell receptors from receiving signals that tell them to divide and grow. The drug is a mouse, yes, MOUSE, antibody that has been changed to make it similar to a human antibody. It is likely that my body will develop additional antibodies that will prevent the effectiveness of future mouse-based therapies. I'm not certain if this will affect my desire or ability to go to Disney World or view Fantasia.

Debbie mentioned that everyone in the study has developed an acne-like rash on the face, and some have it on the chest and back. Fatigue and low blood counts are frequent side effects. Nausea and hair loss, however, have been rare. There are fifteen other people in this study. I think that makes me Sweet Sixteen.

I've enjoyed this week of increased energy and disappearing rash. I've even been swimming three times. It's difficult to think about walking back into a chemo session knowing that I won't feel this good for the next two months. Hopping onto the Wednesday morning Southwest flight doesn't sound like much fun either (Who wants peanuts at 6:15 am?). Yet, there is some comfort in knowing that something is planned and in the works.

There's certainly no guarantee that the Eribtux will work for me. A woman in my support group mentioned that she was on different chemo treatments for a year until they found her "bullet". I'm thankful that on-going research provides us with options and opportunities.

Yours 'til the mouse traps,

Sarah

April 09, 2008—7:19pm

Greetings from Houston Hobby airport. My flight leaves in about an hour. It has been a long day.

I did get to see Dr. Coleman today. I told him how much I appreciated him listening to me and allowing me time to sort all of it out. His response, "Well of course. We're a team. "ahhhh.

My infusion lasted about 5 hours because there was a little hiccup. About 3/4 of the way thru the Erbitux, I started coughing and became really short of breath. It was a little scary, but the nursing staff sprang into choreographed action. In less than 5 minutes I was on oxygen and getting hydrocorto-something on my iv (really glad that the big needle I saw didn't go straight into my arm—Ouch)

The rest of the infusion was delayed, but finally completed. They observed me for an hour following the chemo. I was lucky to be in a bed. Poor Mother had the most boring time. At least I slept.

I'm starting to get a headache and look forward to getting home. If only I could just click my ruby red heels.

Yours 'til the oxygen tanks,

Sarah

If cancer was a crayon,
It would be violet.
The color of a whisper
My shadow's edge
The depths of the universe
Night prying the fingers of day's last grasp.
Hope and despair occupying the same chair.

If cancer was a sound
It would be a leaky faucet
The maddening echo
The thief of sleep
The constant constant
Erosion of my control predictable yet hesitant
Consuming cadence longing for distraction.

If cancer was weather
It would be the fog.
Clouding my familiar
The weight of the wait
The slowly lifted veil
An engulfing atmosphere of sudden solitude
Tearfully blurring edges of light and the known

Cancer is a violet bruise.
Cancer is a leaky optimism.
Cancer is a foggy journey.
I can live with that.

Yours 'til the crayon boxes,

Sarah

April 16, 2008—9:49pm

THE GOOD
- Chemo only lasted two hours, and there was no allergic reaction.
- I caught an earlier flight and was home before 6:30 pm

THE BAD
- Mother was kind enough to bring some Amish Friendship bread for a snack in the car. Ick. No wonder the Amish don't have more friends.
- I was too tired and had no appetite for my great lunch at Café Rabelais.

THE UGLY
- The first painful stick for the iv made my blood vessel bulge and burn. The inside of my left wrist is blue and purple.
- The anticipated rash has arrived. Red spots are mainly on my chest but moving up the chins and around my mouth.

Yours 'til the wrist watches,

Sarah

April 19, 2008—8:18pm

During my junior high summers, my friend Wendy and I would walk or ride our bikes to the 7-Eleven to spend our 26 cents on Spree packages and Icees. It was somewhat of a long trip along a busy 4 lane road. One day I spied a sandal in the road that had been run over by several cars. I picked it up and immediately knew that it was my shoe.

It was a Thom McCann t-strap white leather sandal, and it was my exact size. The telltale stitching from the repair shop was present (I had tripped and consequently ripped the middle in-between-the-toes thong out of the shoe.) I took the sandal home, and found its mate in my closet. I have no earthly idea how my sandal could have ended up a mile away from my house. It's one of the mysteries of life. In fact, for years, I have stated that the first thing I plan to ask God is, "How did my sandal get in the road?"

(One time in college, Charles was participating in a spiritual discussion group and the topic of "What would you ask God?" was brought up. How nice of Charles to share my sandal story with the group. A few years ago, we were driving to the Chimayo chapel in New Mexico, and we saw a child's white sandal in the middle of the road. It does the soul good to laugh that hard.)

I'm still sticking with that as my first question, but my next question for God is probably going to be "What was I supposed to learn from my cancer experience?"

I just can't help thinking that I'm missing something.

I've certainly learned more about patience and letting go and accepting things for what they are. I understand more about priorities and that time, like money, should be spent wisely. I am able to better distinguish between the treasures found in the common and the trivial in the monumental. I've experienced kindness beyond measure and the deepest respect for the human spirit. And, boy, I have gotten countless laughs from the cast of cancer.

I've also learned that many areas need growth in my life. I still waste time and energy with worry and often allowed myself to become overwhelmed. (The bumper crop of rash zits on my face is my latest.) I'm selfish sometimes, and I know that I'm not giving as much of myself as many loved ones need. I tend to distance myself at times. I know that many of my expectations are unrealistic.

However, I feel that there is something else…something important… that is just beyond my grasp. Until that veil is lifted, I guess I'm just supposed to keep on going. Maybe that's the purpose of the whole "I'm Not Finished" mindset. Maybe it is.

Yours 'til the sandal straps,

Sarah

— ~ —

April 24, 2008—10:35am

> **obstacle course:** *n. A series of challenging physical obstacles an individual or team must navigate usually while being timed.*

I didn't expect the rash to make the insertion of my iPod earbuds difficult, but it has. The army of red zits has spread past my eyebrows and forehead and is now in my hair. They (chile) pepper my chest and back, and yes, have even found my ears.

Debbie, the clinical study nurse, told me that the rash wasn't bad enough to delay treatment by one or two weeks, like some people do. Yowza! I don't want to do that. I can't imagine flying down to Houston one Wednesday and being told that the rash is too severe for chemo. They gave me a prescription ointment. It won't clear up the zits, but hopefully it will take away some of the painful and ever-present irritation.

All in all, chemo went pretty well yesterday. I got in early, slept through most of the treatment, and had a great lunch with Mother at Benjy's (I highly recommend it.) The only concern was my very LOW blood pressure during the infusion. Trust me, it's not a result of being overly relaxed. The nurses monitor me for an hour after treatment, and I was back to a normal reading by then.

The whole Love Field Hobby MDA and so forth has a bit of a "herding cattle" feeling to it. Even though I'm moving, there's a passive quality to the whole thing. It's a struggle for an independent person to go through the motions, the protocols, the procedures, the waiting, waiting, waiting.

I'm fortunate to have pleasant people along the way. The lighthearted Southwest employees have only had one grump in my three weeks of travel, and the healthcare staff has been exceptional. I'm even becoming more adjusted to Mother's defensive driving shuttle service. (However, one lane change and/or possible seizure was questioned yesterday.)

Today is that post chemo blah fatigue blah headache blah stomach scene. Another hurdle that I'll make it over.

Yours 'til the cattle calls,

Sarah

❦

April 26, 2008—2:33pm

I don't have pets. I used to say that I had 5th graders, so I didn't need pets. I consider myself more of a dog person than a cat person, and we had dogs when I was growing up.

I have been amazed at the results I've witnessed at Baylor's pet therapy sessions. Volunteers bring in trained and screened dogs to the various waiting room areas. The handler is good at reading which patients are interested in visiting with the dogs. I've seen some patients light up like a Christmas tree. You can tell that it really makes their day.

I got my prescription ointment for my rash last Thursday. It's called clindamycin and it's more of a lotion than ointment. I put a thin film on the affected areas 2x a day. The rash is not going away, but it seems to be getting a little less irritated (and irritating). The lotion has an odd odor that was slightly repulsive and vaguely familiar. It took a couple days to figure out the smell.

I don't know if anyone else remembers Gaines burgers. They were mealy smelly dog food formed into a hockey puck "burger" shape and wrapped in cellophane. You crumbled them up into your dog's bowl. Yep, it's the same smell. It's a variation on that smell that lets me know I've wandered too far away from the household goods department in Target. I always try to take a deep breath and hold it as I walk past the pet food aisle in the grocery store, too. Now, I'm smearing that smell on my face, chest and back twice a day.

> So, just to sum up.
> Pet therapy = good.
> Pet food face therapy = bad.

Hope you're enjoying a great weekend.
Yours 'til the dog bowls,

> ### Sarah

PS—-Charles was kind enough to say, "Your rash doesn't look QUITE as bad as you think." For everyone's sake I'm not including pictures of my back, neck, or ears.

May 01, 2008—9:26am

> ### *I am not in the giving vein to-day.*
> ### Shakespeare, Richard III

When I first started chemo (can we believe it's been nearly a year already?), Dr. Coleman told me that getting a port was an option for me, but since it can be a source of infection, he suggested that I try doing the regular I.V. needle in the vein approach. I would have three weeks between each treatment, so I could probably stand it.

Yesterday was my (lucky?) 13th chemo. I was sent to the I.V. team to get my line started since the nurses have been having trouble finding a good vein to use for treatment. Still, I required two sticks to get the needle in correctly. I usually don't watch, but yesterday I was sitting up and my arm was on the table in front of me. I made the mistake of looking at the starter needle.

I've realized that although the initial stick does hurt, what really bothers me is feeling them work the needle and tubing through the vein. Now that I'm getting treatment on a weekly basis, it seems to be more and more difficult. The nurse pushes on the vein from the outside while the needle is inserted to get the thing lined up. My veins seem to meander (like my stories?) and they need a straight shot.

It's hard for me to sit still, and most of the time it makes me cry. Each session begins with an infusion of Benadryl, then the Erbitux. Often the Benadryl is slightly cold and while it doesn't burn, there is an awful feeling when it goes through my vein. I feel some arthritis-like aching around the infusion area. My best days occur when sleep comes quickly with the Benadryl. I'm happy that all the rooms at MDA have beds. Luckily, I didn't get a horrible bruise last like week, (Love the Gorbachev suggestion, B.H.), but my arm is very tender today.

I discussed all of this with my clinical research nurse, Debbie, and she is going to check with Dr. Coleman to see if I need to get a port. During an outpatient surgery, a catheter is inserted under the skin into a vein in my neck or chest. Nurses can access the port easily and I will feel the stick of an injection rather than the spelunking of late.

The idea of yet another surgical procedure stirs up many feelings. I don't know if it would be done in Houston or Dallas. I haven't heard anything definitive from Debbie or Dr. Coleman (I do see him next week). Lots of "don't knows". What else is new? We shall see.

Thanks for all the fun trip names. Mother and I got a good laugh from the list.

Yours 'til the port whines,

Sarah

PS—Happy May, enjoy this month's "international flavor" family
photo.

May 04, 2008—7:20pm

We've all been there. It's a part of our shared existence. A trip to
the Department of Motor Vehicles is always unpleasant.

> The forms.
> The lines
> The hidden "take a number" dispenser
> The terrapin (tortugian?) pace
> The bad lighting
> The smell
> The hairstyles

It seems particularly unkind that the trip should also include a
disturbing glimpse at one's own mortality.

> Tick.
>> Tick.
>>> Tick.

Most days I don't think about dying from cancer. I make efforts
to focus on living with cancer. Cancer is not the death sentence that
it once was. Medical advances have been significant. Perhaps my
clinical trial will be of benefit to me and many others as well.

However sometimes, the possibility……..the reality……....the
probability……… of the journey's end smacks me right in the face.
I just didn't expect the slapping to come from the blue disability
parking placard. Ouch.

Wednesdays have proven to be very long days. I don't have any
extra energy when I leave MDA after chemo, and after tackling

both airports, well, I can just barely make it to the car at Love Field. As fatigue becomes more and more a permanent fixture in my life, it makes sense to avoid further taxing my system.

Deciding to get a handicapped-parking permit was a threshold that I found hard to cross. Seeing the box for "Permanent Disability" checked on the form didn't make it any easier, and getting the placard that is good until May 2012 just pushed me over the edge. That date seems so distant and unimaginable. I don't even know whether we're going to call it twenty-twelve or two thousand twelve. And then the big question........will I expire before the placard does?

A positive attitude doesn't make it through each and every day. Living in the moment is often difficult, and it's nearly impossible to prevent the darkness from seeping in sometimes. Doubts and worries can't always be kept at bay. That's the way it is. The challenge is to tip the scales away from what weighs most on our minds. Different days bring different levels of success in that endeavor.

I called Charles on my way out of the DMV and made it to the car before I started crying. He wondered how long I planned on crying because he thought maybe we could meet for lunch. God love that guy.

Yours 'til the parking spaces,

Sarah

PS I am getting a port. I'll go to Houston to meet with anesthesia and do the procedure the following day. I'm not sure if they can get me in this week, but we're trying.

May 12, 2008—3:56pm

One of my chemo nurses had told me that some patients experience problems with their nails as a result of treatment. I had been pretty lucky until about a week ago. My nails are brittle and thin and have started to crack. The skin around the nails is dry and splitting, and I've been wearing Band-Aids on five fingers (that's half!) Of course it only hurts when you touch something (or type), and that's always.

It doesn't take very long for the fabric Band-Aids to discolor and fray and look disgusting. Last Friday night as I walked through the rain along the streets of New York's Lower East Side, I realized that all I needed was a couple of black teeth and a tattered top hat, and I could star as Fagin in Oliver Twist.

Thanks to Maggie B., I've discovered all of the Burt's Bees hand and nail repair items (including cotton gloves). I look so dainty typing away right now.

Weekly chemo has given me a new definition of fatigue. I go to bed tired and wake up tired. Sometimes I'm too tired to walk. Sometimes I'm too exhausted to sit up. Often, I'm too fatigued to focus. I am never NOT tired. It just varies in degrees. I'm working to find a livable balance for this "newest normal."

It was great to see everyone in New York, and the weather was perfect on Saturday and Sunday. I wish I could have done more, but I'm realizing my limitations. I am proud to say that I made it up to Stephanie's 4th floor walk up on two different days. (I'm not saying how long it took, however.) Her over-the-top dinner party on Friday night was worth every step.

I was almost asleep on Friday afternoon when the M.D. Anderson scheduling nurse called with an update. I'm having my port placement done on May 28th. The date coincides with my 8th week of this clinical trial, and I'll have scans the following week. We're hoping that the Erbitux is working. If so, I'll have more infusions. If not, Dr. Coleman will return to his long list of other possible treatments. Either way more chemo will be in my future, and I'll appreciate the ease that the port provides.

All in all I have fourteen appointments at M.D. Anderson (ranging from tests to chemotherapy to surgery) in the next 23 days. I must remember that two weeks after that last appointment, I'll be heading to Hawaii to see my nieces and blended siblings. It all seems quite overwhelming, but I'm trying to put the AUNT back into UNDAUNTED.

Yours 'til the mani cures,

Sarah

꠷ ꠶

May 15, 2008—12:42pm

Perhaps we all know this story.

It had been raining for days and days, and a terrible flood had come over the land. The waters rose so high that one man was forced to climb onto the roof of his house.

As the waters rose higher and higher, a man in a rowboat appeared, and told him to get in. "No," replied the man on the roof. "I have faith in the Lord, the Lord will save me." So the man in the rowboat went away.

The man on the roof prayed for God to save him.

The waters rose higher and higher, and suddenly a speedboat appeared. "Climb in!" shouted a man in the boat. "No," replied the man on the roof. "I have faith in the Lord; the Lord will save me." So the man in the speedboat went away.

The man on the roof prayed for God to save him.

The waters continued to rise. A helicopter appeared and over the loudspeaker, the pilot announced he would lower a rope to the man on the roof. "No," replied the man on the roof. "I have faith in the Lord, the Lord will save me." So the helicopter went away.

The man on the roof prayed for God to save him.

The waters rose higher and higher, and eventually they rose so high that the man on the roof was washed away, and alas, the poor man drowned.

Upon arriving in heaven, the man marched straight over to God. "Heavenly Father," he said, "I had faith in you, I prayed to you to save me, and yet you did nothing. Why?"

God gave him a puzzled look, and replied "I sent you two boats and a helicopter, what more did you expect than that?"

~~~~~~~~~~~~~~~~~~~~~~~~

I've been thinking about this story a lot lately. I have complete faith in the power of God, and I believe that nothing is beyond His reach. That faith comforts me with the knowledge that no matter how this turns out, I will be okay. However, the unknown aspects, as well as the physical components, comprise my on-going struggle. I believe that opportunities are presented to me and then I have choices to make. I've mentioned to others that difficulty comes with trying to decide which boat I am meant to board.

The boat story also makes me think of the victims of the recent disasters in Myanmar and China. I think of all the people who wonder if anyone is able to come to their aid. Such fear, loss, and hopelessness are too immense to fully comprehend. I pray that governments facilitate rather than hinder humanitarian aid. I was able to make a donation for relief efforts at www.redcross.org. I figure it's one small way to be part of the solution.

In contrast, there are so many visions of hope for me. I find encouragement all around me, even in the midst of the struggle. Yesterday's MDA visit was physically draining. The ultrasound technician pushed so hard on my abdomen that I feared a bone (rib or pelvic) might crack, however, the test revealed no further accumulation of fluid. My man Omar was successful with the backside of my arm for IV placement, and my infusion was completed without incident. It was a very long day, but Mother was able to move me to a later flight without too much trouble. I'm home, sore and bruised from my day, but safe and sound. The strength and assistance needed to make it through these times continues to be given to me. For that, I'm truly grateful.

Yours 'til the deck hands,

Sarah

May 16, 2008—12:18pm

I was the youngest person at our table last night during the birthday celebration dinner, yet I was the only one who had to get the car keys about 2/3 of the way through the meal so I could go lie down in the car. I was simply too tired to sit up. It's very frustrating, and I often feel that I'm going through all of this treatment but I'm still missing out on so much. (Especially when I know that my companions are going to be talking about me, and I won't be there to zing them back with clever retorts.)

A range of emotions is always present. I believe the trick is recognizing the feelings, but not letting the emotions control you. Let's see if you can match up the emotional responses in these following situations from last evening.

1. On the drive over, Charles mentions that he's started worrying about getting cancer because "I think I might have been exposed to asbestos when I did construction work for three days in Austria in 1986."
    a. Deep concern
    b. Compassion (from one cancer survivor to another)
    c. Eye rolling "Give me a break" disbelief
    d. Curiosity (as in "I wonder who sings that song that is playing on the radio; oh, were you saying something, Charles?")

2. Upon sitting down at the table, Mary says, "You look pretty good for one day after chemo."
    a. Pride in my appearance

b. Grateful for the ambient lighting and Mary's poor eyesight

c. Embarrassment (Does this mean she can see the sticky spot on this shirt left by the size label? I pinned the jacket strategically so it wouldn't show.)

d. Insecurity (....pretty good for ONE DAY after chemo. How bad must I look for just normal?)

3. Returning from my baby nap in the car just in time to see Dan and Charles holding hands and arms across the table.

a. Anxiety because they must certainly be discussing Charles' possible melanoma on his arm. (Yes, worried about ANOTHER cancer.)

b. Disappointment over not having a camera ready.

c. Delight because now I KNOW they're not talking about me.

d. More delight since I plan to write about this on the CarePage.

Yours 'til the feeling's mutual,

Sarah

PS—Happy belated birthday to Dan!

May 22, 2008—12:20pm

I believe that flexibility was one of my strengths as a teacher. It involves a "letting go" that was seldom a problem for me. Perhaps that ability sprouts from the comfort of familiarity and experience. We are more resistant to change-more inflexible-when things are unfamiliar or overwhelming.

Yesterday at MDA was a whirlwind and a true test of tenacity and patience. My first appointment was at 7:30 am, and we walked out just after 4:00 pm. During that time I met with 12 individual healthcare providers.

The stress of the day was compounded when I found out that I would probably NOT be getting my port placement next Wednesday as planned. The surgeon, Dr. Brown, did not want me to have scans so soon after placement. A patient lies on the CT scan track with both arms above his/her head during the procedure. Such arm movement can dislodge the catheter in the vein.

Great, I have all these pre-placement meetings (anesthesia, surgical, etc.) scheduled and now I can't do it. The CT scans must be done along the clinical trial timetable. I feel so removed from the decision process. It's often hard to act, but even harder to feel so acted upon.

Later I find out that they can switch the surgery to the day AFTER my scans. I'll be meeting with Dr. Coleman that day, but they'll have the procedure done prior to that appointment. My pre-placement appointments can continue and all is well.

However, I learn that I am not allowed to swim for six weeks following the surgery. I'll be in Hawaii for 10 days and not be able to get into the water. This revelation was quite upsetting. Most cancer patients wrestle with treatment and quality of life issues. When is enough enough? When does the treatment for prolonging life overshadow the living of life itself? I have already accepted that my vacation will be limited by fatigue and an increased sensitivity to the sun. It takes me a while to get my head wrapped around all of this.

Wait! The rash on my chest!! Dr. Brown is very meticulous, and the rash is a concern. Will the rash continue to clear and be better in two weeks? Who knows? (Dr. Brown is quite something. He has done over 4000 port placements and only about 1% have had any complications. He went over the consent forms line by line with me, and I have to give him credit because he didn't even flinch when Mother mentioned that she was an attorney. He told us that the nurses note "The doctor does NOT like to be rushed.")

It was also suggested that I wait until after Hawaii to have the port implanted. That was disturbing news. I've been waiting since early April for this procedure, and it keeps being postponed. This is where the unfamiliarity affects flexibility. The mention of another delay left me grasping and unnerved. We left with the placement tentatively scheduled for June 4th after my scans and before my meeting with Dr. Coleman. I walked out of MDA feeling tired and tense.

I feel that my first reaction is very much part of the human condition. When things are spinning out of our control, we tend to try to control ANYTHING we can. We become inflexible because another change is just too much. We get wrapped up in righteousness and protocol rather than common sense and listening. We yell at both the car that cut in front of us, and at the driver that won't let us cut in front of him.

Stepping back from the ordeal of the day, it now seems best to postpone the surgery until after my trip. Why not enjoy the vacation to the best of my ability? It will mean another stick or two for chemo infusions, but I can make it through that. I am part of the decision-making team in my treatment plan. That's a much better place to be. I've talked to MDA, and I'll get a later date scheduled probably early July.

Yours 'til the consent forms,

Sarah

PS—Sophia visited for Sarah's (Papania) graduation last weekend. The crew came over for dinner on Monday. She was a trooper during a busy, busy weekend.

May 30, 2008—10:00am

After only 20 something flights, I've about gotten this Southwest Airlines gig down pat. Here are the important things to know:

- Southwest still has open seating—no seat assignments, however, you must check in to get your coveted place in line.
- I've mastered the day early alert on my iPhone and am consistently in the A boarding group ("…sometimes even less than 30," she gleefully whispered)
- I like to grab my seat belt extension and an aisle seat near the front. It's a tricky operation, however human beings have this wonderful quality of searching for something better, and I'm taking full advantage. Only a rare individual will take the middle seat in the front of the plane and abandon the possibility down the aisle. It's sort of my own "Deal or No Deal."
- The early morning and late afternoon flights are usually completely full, so often there's no chance for an open middle seat, but when there is just that small glimmer of hope…well, I've hit the jackpot.
- The winning avoidance combination is a big girl (me) and a child (an unaccompanied minor traveling alone or better yet, a mother with a baby on her lap.) Trust me, NO businessman wants to take THAT middle seat. If there is only one seat left open on the entire plane….that will be it.
- I believe the chest and face rash only add to the "Keep Walking" feel of the encounter. What can be said? It's not always the "Friendly Skies".

Despite the on-going fatigue, this Wednesday was fairly easy. Did I ever in my wildest dreams think that I would call a Houston chemo trip "EASY"? This completed the 8 rounds of the Erbitux trial. I go next Tuesday for blood work and scans, and then I'll hear the results from Dr. Coleman on Wednesday. They've already scheduled a chemo session after my appointment with him, so if it's working (and that means the WATT brothers have shrunk, remained the same, or not grown more than 20%), then I'll go for more Erbitux. If the trial has not been successful, then Dr. Coleman will suggest further treatment. I've seen his list. We've got options.

If worrying about next week's results was fruitful, then I'd suggest that we all do it. However, worry won't change a thing, so I'm trying to focus my energies elsewhere.

Either way, I'm looking forward to a little break during my Hawaii trip. I believe once you add the fresh pineapple juice to the Malibu rum then you've entered the health drink zone. (and I think that little umbrella falls into the skin care category).

Yours 'til the flight plans,

Sarah

June 04, 2008—3:44pm

Sarah is on her way back to Dallas and asked me to post an update from her trip to MDA today.

Unfortunately, the Erbitux clinical trial was not successful. However, Sarah will be starting a new type of chemo in Dallas.

Dr. Coleman will be talking with Dr. Koon to determine the best plan. Please continue to keep Sarah in your prayers. She will post more details later.

thanks, Mary

June 05, 2008—7:54am

Tuesday and Wednesday were horribly long days at MDA. The waiting, waiting, waiting is so draining. Yesterday's appointment with Dr. Coleman was scheduled for 11:00. I finally went back into the exam room at 12:30, waited until 1:20 to see his fellow, Dr. Kamat, and then waited until nearly 2:00 to see Dr. Coleman. After the physical exam and preliminary reports, Mother and I waited some more for Dr. Coleman to come into the conference area with us. He's really something. He took all the time we needed and went over my CT scans in great detail with us, answered question after question, and made us both laugh.

Even though the wait tries the patience, he is worth the wait. I'm sure he gives every patient the attention, time, and comfort that he always provides for me. He never approaches my cancer as a crisis or something to fear. He has his "laundry list" of things to try next. He offers many suggestions, possible solutions, and definitely hope.

The scan shows that two of the three tumors have grown. They've almost doubled in size. (The largest is about 6 cm, or about three inches.) There are no new tumors present. The past 5 months of treatment (Doxil and then Erbitux) have not been successful in limiting the progression of the disease.

That's about all of the "bad' news. There are so many positive results from yesterday's meeting that will affect my quality of life.

*I will no longer make the weekly trek to Houston. This has been quite a beating for me. I certainly appreciate the Barta's constant hospitality and Mother's unwavering support, but the flights, treatments, and appointments have taken their toll on me.

*I have two weeks without chemo to rest up for my trip to Hawaii. Maybe the rash will go away. Certainly I'll be able to feel more energized and less exhausted. There's a point where treatment for prolonged life can get in the way of living life.

*I was so relieved to hear some of the details from my scan. I've been experiencing tremendous discomfort and pressure in my abdomen and of course my mind had gone all kinds of places with conjecture. I have a herniated area on my right side and some small and large intestine have come through and that causes pressure. A collection of fluid (called ascites) is in my lower pelvis. This fluid is present with the disease. It doesn't hurt anything, but it does cause pressure. When a chemo does start to work, the fluid levels should decrease as well.

*Dr. Coleman and Dr. Koon are so willing to work together. I will see Dr. Koon next week, and I'll get treatment here at Baylor. I'll also have port placement done in Dallas after Hawaii.

*I'm happy to be off the Erbitux. The side effects have really affected my skin. My dry hands are so brittle that yesterday on the plane, two of my fingers started bleeding from the nail beds. (Lucky businessman sitting next to me! I wrapped the fingers up in Kleenex. Of course the only travel pack Kleenex I had have "100% DEVIL" in red letters written on them.)

So, there you have it. The news was disappointing, but I walked away feeling more at ease and happier about the living of my life. Dr. Coleman is suggesting Avastin, which is a very expensive off protocol drug, for my next treatment. He doubts the insurance company will cover it, but it's worth trying. Avastin would be administered in two or three week cycles and would be available in Dallas. If Avastin is not an option, the docs will discuss the next best treatment plan and get back with me.

I'm doing okay with all of this news. I'm not in a bad place. I'm optimistic about the big picture, and absolutely thrilled about the next four weeks. I guess the abdomen's half empty instead of half full.

Thanks for all of the kind words and support.

Yours 'til the lust's for life,

Sarah Merdian

PS—Note to Houston Hobby airport: Maybe we can rethink the John Denver medley Muzak collection and go with a "didn't die in a plane crash" option.

June 06, 2008—10:59am

I used to call the guy who cuts my hair a "hairdresser", but his new business card reads "Life Stylist." Curtis is a great guy and does a wonderful job, but his new salon is a little too young for me. While I waited, I tried to sit on this funky curved modern chair that required a contortion that my body can no longer achieve. The hair washing (follicular lavage?) station seating requires a lithe breezy seating maneuver rather than a lumbering thud, and I believe the club scene sound system actually changed my pulse.

I ended up having an intense pounding pain in my hip that required me to stop the haircutting, excuse me, Life Styling process, on three separate occasions so I could stand or readjust my leg in an attempt for pain relief. Really, a haircut is not supposed to be such a workout. Of course I felt incredibly old and completely exhausted when I left.

How could I have been so surprised with my fatigue levels? Did I really think that after Houston....one day off a chemo cycle....I would be magically rejuvenated? Today I have taken out the trash, brought the recycling container back in, washed the car and made the Starbucks run for a latte, and I'm already back in bed.

Friends are in town this weekend, there's a great concert on Saturday, and I am trying to balance a sense of enthusiasm and reality. It's so frustrating to be so limited. I hate missing out. Making plans is difficult because I frequently don't know until that very moment whether or not I'm up to doing something.

Everything requires its own sort of patience the airport, the doctor's office, test results, traffic, deli counters, family, stamina, wisdom, self-acceptance, and mindfulness.

Have patience with all things, but chiefly have patience with yourself.

—St. Francis de Sales

Have a wonderful weekend.
Yours 'til the shampoo sinks,

Sarah

June 08, 2008—11:28am

During my teaching career, I learned that it was much more beneficial for all if the parents, student, and teacher felt they were all "on the same side of the table." We were a unified team with a shared goal a child's progress and success.

I learned that we could have the courage and honesty to look at what really WAS at any given moment. A child's performance, struggles, setbacks, and growth could be viewed without a label of good or bad, without judgment, without blame. If we were able to somehow remove the guilt, shame, anger, and emotion from the moment, then we had a better chance of moving forward.

During my last visit with Dr. Coleman, I felt the same thing. We were physically on the same side of the table as he went through my ct scans. He never makes me feel like he's bringing me "bad" news. He tells me, or shows me, what is going on, and we go from there. We share the same goal.

He identified many conditions in my body the hernias, the gallstone, the fluid, the tumors, the kidneys and spoke to how they could make me feel physically. There are conditions to monitor, issues to address, and flaws to dismiss. There was no fear or judgment regarding good, bad, or evil in his delivery. There was no dwelling on the past or "if only" statements. There was nothing to hate and everything to embrace.

Heaven knows I've spent so much of my life attaching emotion to my body. I've felt bad, even felt hatred, about my weight or my looks. I've worried about some unknown condition. I've struggled to be any place and anyone except myself in the present moment. It's been such a waste of time, energy, and effort.

Our worth as individuals is not contingent on perfection. All of us—the 5th graders, the relatives, the strangers, the doctors, our bodies, and our minds are doing the very best that we can to move forward. Sometimes we need to do it alone. Sometimes we need more help. Sometimes we resist. Sometimes we accept. Sometimes we succeed. Sometimes we flounder.

I can't express the peace that I feel with the realization that my cancer is not an evil presence. I've spent a lot of energy fighting it and viewing it as an invader and an enemy. I'm not saying that I'm giving up. I'm just seeing that my unfinished fight is FOR health and wellness of body, spirit and mind. I'm not fighting alone. I'm not relishing all the steps of the process, but I'm willing and able to persevere.

Right at this moment, I am imperfect, worthy, and okay. We all are.

Yours 'til the moment's notice,

Sarah Merdian

with a "didn't die in a plane crash" option.

PS—Speaking of the "present". Thanks to all my KC friends for showering me with such delights, such love.

—◦—

June 13, 2008—8:20am

> *In trying to beat cancer, however, I am competing against myself. Cancer is a part of me, so if I win,*

I also lose. Getting whole, getting well, has to do with oneness. It's not a matter of right or wrong, victory or defeat, not even life or death. It is life vs. nonlife. If I experience wholeness in life, death is not a defeat. If I experience fragmentation in life, then life is not a victory.

John McFarland

Thanks to Alan from Baylor for that quote. I couldn't have said it better.

I saw Dr. Koon yesterday, and he'll talk with Dr. Coleman and they'll come up with a treatment plan to present to me on July 2nd. I'll plan on starting a new chemo then. There has been some discussion about a drug called Avastin. It's expensive and not officially a protocol for my kind of cancer, but we shall see.

I expected my first week without a Houston trip to be fun and carefree. Well, strike that. I'm still dealing with severe hip pain (not cancer related), and I want to get that under control before the long flight to Hawaii. I've had three chiropractic appointments, yet prolonged sitting or standing results in pain.

I took a pain pill yesterday after returning from the doctor's appointment, but I guess not eating beforehand was a mistake. I ended up puking all afternoon and feeling woozy and weak. The fluid pressure in my abdomen is uncomfortable and eating a full meal tends to make it worse, so I have been trying to eat smaller amounts throughout the day. Squeezing in a swim time before the doctor just added to the equation. Overexertion, stress, and hunger are to be avoided for a good reason.

I made it through the difficult afternoon and evening. In moments of despair, I wonder if I'll ever feel better again. I'm getting through those tough times sometimes just five minutes at a time, but that counts for something. Hopefully Friday the 13th will prove to be a better day for me.

Sarah Merdian

I hope everyone has a good weekend. It's going to be a hot one here in Dallas.

Yours 'til the June bugs,

Sarah

~•~

June 15, 2008—8:47pm

I've spent most of the weekend feeling depressed, lost, and sorry for myself. I'm realizing that I am probably more ill than I have been willing to admit.

My abdominal pressure issues are ever present. My hip pain is chronic, and now I've developed some sort of inner ear vertigo thing that leaves me "grabbing the sheets" dizzy when I roll over in bed or stand up. I'm apprehensive about the long flights to Hawaii and uncertain what I'll even be able to do once I get there.

I have a constant struggle to balance hope and reality and this weekend.....well, the schoolyard bully named DESPAIR has been sitting on one end of the seesaw.

I decided to turn on the TV in hopes of finding a diversion, and wouldn't you know that I'm smacked right in the face with none other than EXTREME HOME MAKEOVER. Of course it's about a family fighting against the odds. One son has tremendous medical needs and their home is falling apart, and here I am worried about my first class flights on my Hawaiian vacation

I don't know what has me feeling more ashamed..........my self-centered self pity or that it's Ty Pennington giving me some perspective. Okay, I get it.

It doesn't help with the dizziness, or the hip, or pressure, or the apprehension, but it does help with the outlook.

Happy Father's Day to everyone.

Yours 'til the Ty that binds,

Sarah

~•~

Jul 1, 2008—1:59pm

Hawaii can be heaven and it can be hell.
—Jeff Goldblum

Kauai is a paradise. Beautiful scenery, breathtaking flowers, breezy shores, and big-hearted folk. We stayed in quaint cottage plantation with access to a Big house, pool, and spa. Reunion folks brought all kinds of traditional foods. There was always plenty of laughter and lots of activity. For most. I spent the majority of the trip in my room. I could seldom get more than 10 feet away from a restroom. I battled the Big D of the intestinal tract and all of its ramifications. I seldom got any rest although I was in bed most of the time. I missed out on many fun excursions and activities. I ended up in the local ER to determine whether or not the massive leg swelling was from a DVT related blood clot. (Nope, thank goodness just a burst Baker's cyst never heard of it either.) I needed wheelchair service at the airports. I used Percocet painkillers to make the trip home, and last night I fell in my room and my swollen leg is covered in bruises. Not quite paradise, but I'm no complainer. But everything has it moments. I loved visiting when I could. I got to swim in the pool and the ocean. I got two massages and a much-needed post-chemo facial, and the highlight of the trip was the 50-minute helicopter ride over the island. Simply breathtaking—almost surreal—postcard quality pictures all the way.

I'm meeting with Dr. Koon tomorrow to discuss treatment options. I'm hoping to suggest that we wait a week for chemo so I can get more rested. I seem to also have a nasty sinus infection going on.

I'll keep you posted. Many thanks to my friends and family who went out of their way to take care of me during this trip. Too many c cards were played (not just by me, by the way) to even count. I'm grateful that I'm not going through this alone.

Sarah Merdian

During my trip, my 88-year-old Aunt Doris died in Houston. She was diagnosed with advanced liver cancer just a few weeks ago. I had seen her at dinner during my last MDA visit in early June. Her children, grandchildren, great-grandchildren and extended family and friends will remember her. During my recuperation in Houston last summer, she took the time to make my favorite coconut cake. A coconut tree stood outside our cottage in Kauai, and I thought of her often.

Yours 'til we lei it all down,

Sarah

Jul 2, 2008—11:45pm

No wonder Sarah felt so bad in Hawaii... After she went in for tests today at Baylor, they told her she was in renal failure and she was admitted to the E.R. Sarah was in excruciating pain and didn't feel any relief until they put in a catheter a few hours later and drained some of the fluid. The plan was to do surgery and insert some stents to relieve pressure on the bladder. However, after the fluid drained so quickly, Dr. Koon decided that they would monitor her condition, take more tests in the morning and make a decision at that time. Dr. Koon is leaving on vacation tomorrow, so Dr. Oh, his partner, will be taking over Sarah's care. They are probably going to postpone the chemo since it is especially hard on the kidneys. Sarah was still waiting for a hospital room to be available when I left her at 9:30 this evening. Please keep Sarah in your thoughts and prayers.

Mary

Jul 3, 2008—11:58am

Got a text from Sarah at 3am. They finally had a room available! This morning they told her that there would be no surgical procedure today. They are going to continue monitoring her fluid output and her blood work and re-evaluate tomorrow. Her mother is with her and said that Sarah is still in lots of pain despite the meds and is trying to get some sleep.

Mary

— ~ —

Jul 4, 2008—10:50am

Happy 4th of July! If Sarah stays in Robert's room 709 she will have a great view of the fireworks tonite at Fair Park. (She was told she was being moved to the Hoblitzelle building yesterday, but so far that hasn't happened.) It was amazing to see Sarah interact with her caregivers yesterday. No matter who came into her room, an orderly, a nurse, a blood tec etc., there was always a kind word from Sarah and in 2 minutes flat, she had their life history. Despite the pain she was feeling, she was able to brighten their day. If you stop by to see Sarah, please remember to keep the visit short. She said she was up to seeing some visitors, but only for about 15 minutes at a time. If you stay too long, like Dan did yesterday, she will feel free to look at her watch and said 'tic tock.' At least he didn't trip on any of her tubes this time. (Charles, this is when I am tempted to tell everyone that you almost pulled out her catheter when you were rolling around her bed on the stool...oops was that in my out loud voice?) Hugs and love to Sarah

Mary

— ~ —

Jul 4, 2008—9:30pm

Sarah seems much better today! She was moved from Roberts to Hoblitzelle Room 408 (no view of the fireworks, but there is a nice small sofa) and they removed the iv from her hand. She was given a patch to administer the pain meds in a more efficient way and they are monitoring her fluid intake as her kidneys continue to improve and she continues to guzzle Gatorade per her doctor's orders. Sarah even got to sleep for a short time after the marathon move from one building to the other side of the complex. Let's hope she has a peaceful night.

Mary

—✦—

Jul 6, 2008—11:48am

Sarah has just been released from the hospital and is being sent home today. The doctors are still trying to determine the cause of the kidney problem. Hopefully, Sarah will post more info later today or tomorrow when she feels up to it. Take it easy, Sarah, we are all praying for you!

Mary

—✦—

Jul 9, 2008—11:50am

"Sarah, the blood work shows us that you're in renal failure." Gosh, FAILURE is such a strong word. It summons images of dark dead end passageways rather than fields of opportunity. I believe the education profession has developed better ways to communicate such news. "Your kidneys are not currently performing at their full potential." "The renal reports indicate progress that is below expected grade level." "The uncooperative climate between your kidneys and bladder has lead to a decline in effective task completion." "Your kidneys are struggling to meet benchmark standards, so we believe that additional support is required." In education, we know. We've read the book, seen the posters, perused the memos, and created the banners. Failure is not an option. And luckily for me, my kidneys are doing just fine. I did not require emergency surgery.

The bladder is a different story. After being catheterized in the hospital, an amazing 2 liters of fluid was released. (I was told that 2 liters is the most recognizable metric unit for Americans. I'm here to help.) Imagine the relief that provided. I guess the fluid was affecting my nerves in my legs and abdomen, too. I spent the rest of my hospital visit being monitored for renal output and assisted with pain management. Now that I'm home, I'm finding that digestive issues and pain management are my main focus. I've been told that three days of home rest are required for each day spent in the hospital. I'm so very tired. My progress is slow. Thanks to my @#$%, Charles, and Mary for getting me through the ER process. The pain was excruciating and I can't imagine making it through it without their support.

Everyone's emails, visits, cards, and text messages have been a great source of comfort for me. I appreciate your patience with me; I'm often too tired for more than a 5-minute conversation.

I go to the urologist on Friday. They're going to try to determine if the bladder blockage issue is related to my growing tumor, cancer-related abdominal fluid, or perhaps another cause. Surgery might still be an option. Chemotherapy is tentatively scheduled for next week.

Yours 'til the fail safe,

Sarah

❦

Jul 11, 2008—2:11pm

Sarah just called with an update from her doctor's visit this morning. Dr. Frost is still not sure what is preventing her bladder from working properly, but based on Sarah's condition and the June report from M.D.Anderson (thank goodness her mother saved a copy of it and had a copy in her purse), he wants to put in a stent. Sarah will take some medicine over the weekend to deaden the nerves around the bladder and then have day surgery on Tuesday to have the stent inserted. She is supposed to take out her own catheter on Sunday. The stent will go from her bladder to one of her kidneys. Sarah is very tired from a morning of tests and paperwork (and no pain meds) and is resting at home. Her leg is quite swollen and the doctor said the only thing to get the swelling down (if it is indeed caused by the Baker's cyst), is to walk around.... Sarah says she has

℣

gained 40 pounds of fluid in the past month. Please continue to keep Sarah in your thoughts and prayers.

Mary

—❦—

Jul 12, 2008—3:29pm

Sarah called this morning around 8 am and was on her way to the E.R. The pain was pretty bad and the doctor wanted her to be on an IV.

Sarah is feeling a little better, but she is still waiting in the E.R. for a room to become available. She doesn't feel up to writing on the CarePage, but she does read it, and is very grateful for everyone's prayers.

Mary

—❦—

Jul 12, 2008—11:16pm

Sarah got into a room this evening. She is in Hoblitzelle 421. Surgery has been moved up to tomorrow morning at 9 am instead of Tuesday. Dr. Fine, the urologist on call, will be inserting 2 stents since both kidneys need some help. Her creatinine levels have gone up to 4 which means her kidneys aren't 'performing up to standards'. Sarah's iv was accidentally dislodged during the transfer, and it took a bit of time to get the pain meds started again. (Her meds were already overdue because of the transfer process, which made for a painful few hours.) When we stopped in for a quick visit tonight, she said she was doing 'ok' and that her nurse, Cindy, (who moved here from Cambodia when she was four) was super nice.

Lots of love and prayers to you, Sarah!

Mary

PS—I will post an update after the surgery in the morning. It is supposed to take about an hour.

—❦—

Jul 13, 2008—12:15pm

Sarah is in the recovery room and doing ok after her surgery. The doctor was only able to insert one of the stents, into her right kidney. The severe swelling of her left leg continues and they think it is probably due to 'tumor burden'. The doctor said no chemo this week. We love you Sarah!

Mary

———

Jul 14, 2008—9:27am

Sarah saw Dr. Frost this morning and he ordered a renal ultrasound of the left kidney. He also said they might do the 'tube out the back' procedure tomorrow.

More later Mary

———

Jul 15, 2008—10:00am

After running some tests, Dr. Frost said Sarah's kidneys were working fine. She will do some physical therapy today and work on pain management. She has been moved to room 428. Yesterday was difficult for Sarah due to all the tests. They had to tape her legs together for one of tests and it was very painful. The six techs and residents who were helping were especially compassionate, sincere and kind to Sarah. She is very thankful for the wonderful care she is receiving.

Thanks, Mary

———

Jul 15, 2008—9:31pm

Sarah got more information this afternoon. The tests show that her kidneys continue to improve, but they are not strong enough for chemo at this point. During the past 6 weeks, the two tumors have grown into one larger tumor, and it measures about 21 cm. (size of a small cantaloupe). Sarah is glad to know the reason for the discomfort she has been feeling. Dr. Koon returns tomorrow and will talk with Sarah about the next step in her treatment plan. Surgery does not seem to be an option right now. (The recovery from surgery would delay having chemo.) It has been very draining for Sarah in the past few days with all the doctor visits, specialists, and testing procedures, and she thinks it would be best to postpone having visitors until things calm down a bit. Sarah says thanks to everyone who has provided such great care-friends, family and hospital staff. Hugs and prayers to Sarah

Mary

PS—Sarah says having a birthday on the 21st and a tumor that measures 21 would be lucky if she were in Vegas...

——◦——

Jul 20, 2008—9:57pm

Sarah would like to write this note personally but she spent all day preparing for a procedure on her colon tomorrow. She knows it is last minute, but she would like everyone to join her for a special birthday party tomorrow at Baylor Hospital, Hoblitzelle, Room 428 4:30-7:30 Open house. Come and go as you can. You don't need to bring a thing. No alcohol due to Baylor policy. No presents please. Convenient parking on Floyd St. (between Swiss and Gaston off of Washington), or valet for $5 at front door (one block east of Gaston on Washington).

Charles & Dan

——◦——

Jul 23, 2008—8:05pm

Greetings from Room 428 in Baylor's Hoblitzelle Hospital. I've been wanting to add an update for some time, but there have been many turning points in my health. I hope to be able to post more details later.

Due to the current condition of my kidneys, chemotherapy is no longer an option for me. Rather than spending my time fighting cancer, I'm choosing to spend my time living my life. My care is a team approach addressing all my needs. I have experts in areas of oncology and urology as well as palliative care (pain management), nutrition, and physical and occupational therapy. My team will now include hospice. Rest is my daily goal. My multiple procedures and conditions have been nearly overwhelming. I will most likely be in the hospital for another 5 or 6 days. I am monitored in multiple areas and my body needs time to recover. Sitting up is difficult and painful for me, so visits with friends are seldom over 10 or 15 minutes. I'm grateful for the support and assistance that I have received.

My impromptu hospital birthday party was delightful. Who knew you could have colon surgery in the morning and chocolate cake the same evening. Over sixty friends, family, and Baylor employees (including Dr. K) helped me celebrate turning forty-eight. Luckily my pain meds made the Gemmy birthday hamster easier to handle.

Yours 'til the cake walks,

Sarah

Jul 30, 2008—9:23pm

> *Be it ever so humble, there's no place like home.*
> **John Howard Payne**

I was laughing during my catheter replacement.
I was overwhelmed with being outside today.
I was crying during my ambulance ride home.
I am living.
I am dying.
I am home.

August 5, 2008—7:33pm

Cards and Letters

If Sarah has ever helped you in your life, please send her a card and let her know how special she is to you.

Her address is:

    4727 Capitol Ave

    Dallas, TX 75204

Also, if you know someone that doesn't read the CarePage, but would like to be included, please notify them.

Thanks, Mary

—~ ~—

August 7, 2008—2:21pm

Dear Friends of Sarah

It is with a heavy heart that I post the news that Sarah passed away this afternoon, around 1 p.m.

For the past two days Sarah has drifted in and out of consciousness, but had her lucid moments. Yesterday she told us that she was 'ready to go' and Msgr. Don Fischer held a beautiful prayer service around her bedside and we all held hands with Sarah. She was unable to take pills anymore, and was given liquid morphine to make her as comfortable as possible.

I will post details about the Memorial Service as they become available.

Love to Sarah

Mary

—~ ~—

August 7, 2008—11:26pm

Celebration of Life

The Celebration of Sarah's life will be held on Sunday, August 17th in the late afternoon and the Memorial Service will be Monday morning, August 18th at St. Joseph's Catholic Church in Richardson, TX. More details to follow.

Love to Sarah in her new home.

Mary

~——~

August 10, 2008—3:55pm

SARAH'S OBITUARY

Sarah Mae Merdian b. July 21, 1960 in Houston, Texas. d. August 7, 2008 in Dallas, Texas.

Sarah inspired everyone with her zest for living and her sense of humor. She was a Master Teacher and empowered lifelong learners through her many years of service as a fifth grade teacher. Sarah truly loved her students and made lasting impacts on their future. She enjoyed seeing the world and continued traveling even as she battled endometrial cancer with trips to China, the Czech Republic and Hawaii.

Sarah graduated from the University of Dallas with a B.A. in History in 1982, a B.A. in Elementary Education in 1983 and an M.A. in Education from St. Mary's College in Kansas in 1997.

Sarah started her career at St. Cecilia's Catholic School in Dallas and worked at Clinton P. Russell Elementary in D.I.S.D, East Antioch and Arrowhead Elementary Schools in the Shawnee Mission District in Kansas City, and more recently at Peak Preparatory in East Dallas. Her humor and love of children will be dearly missed.

Preceded in death by her father Anton W. Merdian, step mother Mary Lou Merdian, and Aunt Doris Housewright. Survived by her mother, M. Jane Merdian, Sister Monica Lynn Stephen. Aunts and

Uncles, Sister Mary Merdian O.S.M., Frances Fontaine, Joyce Pilgreen and John Merdian. Step brothers and sisters, Shannon and Laureen Lunsford, Scott and Heidi Lunsford, Brenda and Steve Peterson.

Special thanks to her caregivers and medical teams at Baylor Medical Center, Dallas, M.D. Anderson in Houston, Vitas Hospice and friends at Gilda's House in Dallas.

Wake Service begins at 4:30 p.m. on August 17th at St. Joseph's Catholic Church, 600 S Jupiter Rd, Richardson, TX. Mass of the Resurrection will be held at St. Joseph's at 10:30 a.m. on Monday, August 18th.

Blessed to have been able to share in a part of her incredible life! May God comfort you in this time of immeasurable loss.

END NOTES

[1] "Fireworks." Schoolhouse Rocks. *Season 3: American Rock.* ABC. 1977 Video. www.schoolhouserock.tv.

[2] Rodgers, Jimmie. "Peach Pickin' Time Down In Georgia." Father of Country Music, Pearl.

[3] "Buddha in the Waiting Room" Paul Brenner. Beyond Words Publishing Inc. 2002. ISBN: 1-582-70-06-X.

[4] Jagger, Mick. & Richards, Keith. "You Can't Always Get What You Want." Grounded for Life. Decca Records, 1969.

[5] Morrison, Van. "The Mystery." The Best of Van Morrison, Volume 2. Polydor. 1993. (Sarah was listening to this music when she left this world.)

[6] Petty, Tom. "The Waiting." Hard Promises. Backstreet Records. 1981.

Afterword

Charles Osterman

Time plus tragedy equals comedy. It's a line that I learned from Sarah that comes from a Woody Allen film. She would remind me of that line when I was overwhelmed or discouraged, and I think it reveals something about how Sarah approached the world.

Anyone who knew Sarah knew the multifaceted person she was. Sarah, the intellect, Sarah, the comedian, Sarah, the teacher and guide, Sarah, the independent, Sarah, the caretaker, Sarah, the voice of reason (cooking spoiled chicken or ham will not make it edible, Charles), Sarah, the good friend, Sarah, the sister and daughter, Sarah, the story teller.

Whoever Sarah was, whatever Sarah did, it was always sweetened with her humor and her stories. The day she found out she might have cancer, she called me. It started like any other phone call, and she asked how my day was going and, of course, I had to let her know. I was at the gas station pumping gas; the catch on the nozzle wouldn't work; I had to stand there the entire time and hold the nozzle; it was hot; I still had errands to run, and my afternoon just wasn't going well.

SILENCE

And then I hear: "They think I might have cancer."

There were tears, the errands were forgotten, I rushed over to her house and Dan and I spent the evening with her listening and consoling. I don't remember who called her later, but I do remember Sarah's rendition of the afternoon "I might have cancer, and, oh, and by the way, Charles is having a bad day, too, because he had to hold the gas pump b/c it wouldn't catch."

Time plus tragedy equals comedy

It didn't matter if it was mundane, or if it was seemingly off limits—Sarah would eventually find humor in it. When her father died, she was absolutely devastated, but it didn't take long before Sarah started working through it with her humor. She let it be known she had a theory on what had happened: it was her sister, Monica's fault. He had visited Sarah in KC about a month before his death and everything had been fine. He went to Tulsa for Thanksgiving and ate dinner at Monica's was it too much pepper in the green beans or turkey that was undercooked? A week later he's dead. What else could one assume?

Time plus tragedy equals comedy

Towards the end of her illness, Sarah reached a point where she didn't want to take her pills anymore. The nurse and I were coaxing her, and after we finally convinced her to take them, she announced, "Laura promised me something sweet and that wouldn't be either of you two."

Time plus tragedy equals comedy

Through these stories and laughs, Sarah drew us all into her world, and we became a part of her, and she a part of us. People who had never even met her responded to her entries on her CarePage. Her beauty of spirit, her depth of character, and her open and inviting heart let each of us share a special connection with her. Mike Greaven, a UD classmate, liked to tease her and say they would put on her tombstone:

"She died of too much affection."

It could have been true. We all loved Sarah. We all took joy in her life. And knowing Sarah and how she lived, I think she would challenge us to find some joy in her death.

In closing, I want to share a quote from A.A. Milne that describes sentiments I think Sarah would want us all to believe in, words I think she lived by, and now lives on by.

> *If ever there is tomorrow when we're not together… there is something you must always remember. You are braver than you believe, stronger than you seem, and smarter than you think. But the most important thing is, even if we're apart…*
>
> *I'll always be with you.*

Sister Mary Merdian, SSMN

Dear Sarah,

I am so glad that you gave permission to your Mother to have your CarePages shared with others. You taught us so much about living and dying through your reflections, your honesty and your humor. You bravely faced and accepted your cancer and I know that the book will help others through their ups and downs as they face the disease.

Sarah, I am especially grateful to God for the time I was with you as your principal at St. Cecilia School. I did not have a lot of time to get to know you while you were growing up. Therefore, it was a special experience for me to get to discover you as an adult.

You were such a fantastic teacher and a marvelous person to have on a faculty. You loved your students and planned so many learning adventures for them. Yes, I know that your classroom was always a mess, but there were so many projects to help the children to learn. Your classes were so creative and fun; your students loved you and imitated you as they grew.

You were always a wonderful team player with the other faculty members. You knew when your humor was needed and when others needed a pat on the back. I loved the joy and surprises you provided (like that exotic hairstyle you arrived with one morning); you understood the meaning of Christianity in your relations with others. You loved your family and made wonderful plans to keep in touch. I will always be grateful for the time you spent with my Mother after Daddy died. You listened and helped her through those first days of being alone.

Sarah, Christmas is fast approaching. I especially miss your Christmas cards made with pictures from your world travels. My favorite is the one in the old European train station with its glass roots and hanging baskets.

Sarah, thank you for sharing yourself with all of us. I miss you and love you very much!

From one of your "Favorites",

Sister Mary Merdian, SSMN

Emily Tamblyn

On Thursday after I found out about Sarah's passing, I stood up from my desk in a kind of daze and hit my knee really hard. In my head, I heard Sarah happily offer to step on my foot to distract me.

My name is Emily Tamblyn, and even though I was in Sarah's 5th grade class 15 years ago, the memories I have of her teaching are still vivid. It was a special year. I was talking to Kim Roembach-Ratliff, who sadly can't be here today, and we were discussing what made Sarah such a great teacher. Kim said to me, that's like asking what makes the sun shine. In the classroom, her enthusiasm for learning and ingenuity for teaching were boundless. In fifth grade, she convinced us that our elementary school was putting a tax on all of our writing instruments, which, in fact, was a clever ruse on her part to give us a taste of the outrage that the Bostonians must have felt when British taxed their tea. By the end of the day, our class was geared up to overthrow the PTA. Sarah always had a way to bring difficult concepts home for her students. Her love of math especially transformed an area of dread for many of us into something we could manage. Many of her students, myself included, who were overwhelmed by math, now count it as one of our strengths. Sarah knew that not all students fit the same mold, and she found new options for learning that cultivated creativity. Teaching was personal for Sarah; every student who went through her class got individual attention that let them know that she believed in her students. And because she believed in us, we succeeded.

Sarah Merdian

Sarah's support extended long after I was officially her student. Her ongoing love and support was a vital thing for me, and for many others. Sarah constantly had former students stopping by to help with her classroom or just to say hi. When I moved to Chicago a few years ago, she was a role model for me as a strong, smart, resourceful woman taking the steps to make a life and a career for herself. I moved to Chicago to pursue theatre, and Sarah sent me a check earmarked to help pay for my first theatre class; she was always looking for ways to encourage students, both past and present.

Sarah said I'm Not Finished, and death has not nullified that motto.

Sarah is absolutely not finished. Trying to count the number of lives that Sarah touched would be futile- it would multiply and multiply again. Sarah taught us to love to learn, to be excited for new things, to find joy in what is around us, to work hard, to love and to show love, and to have a sense of humor in all that we do. I'm going to miss Sarah terribly, but I know that she will never be finished, because we will carry these things with us and we will share them with others. Sarah, we will take you with us where ever we may go.

Christine Garrett

Everyone has a Sarah story. She had a gift for making everyone feel important. We all felt like she was "Our Sarah." She will always be in all of us.

Sarah called me the Saturday before her forty-eighth birthday to ask if I could come to Dallas to help her celebrate her "Last birthday". I was so sad and tearful, but Sarah, always the one comforting said, "Christine, don't worry. I'll always be in you; you'll always be in me. We'll always have one heart."

Sarah and I met when she came to interview for the fifth grade position left vacant by my dear friend Jan Hodgson. She'd left enormous shoes to fill. Mr. Carter allowed me to participate in the interviews. The first candidate was good. The second was better. Then Sarah arrived. She was fashionably dressed in a natural colored linen wrap around dress. (No one here is probably surprised by the fact that I remember what she wore) When we finished her interview, I said, "Well, she's the one. We're finished aren't we?" After she was hired, I invited her over for lunch. Trying to be the good hostess, I played country and western music for my new friend from Texas. She later told me she hates country and western music.

…turns out stereotypes aren't always accurate. Who knew? Sarah did and now that understanding is always in me.

Sarah and I taught twenty feet from each other for twelve years at Arrowhead. We ate lunch together, had recess duty together, study groups, Christmas parties, committees. During her first year, we held a big Rain Forest Celebration as the culminating event for a fourth, fifth and sixth grade unit. Sarah encountered someone she didn't recognize and queried, "Are you the parent of a fourth grader?"

He responded, "No, I'm Gene Johnson, associate superintendent."

Sarah said, "Oh, it's nice to meet you. I'm Christine Garrett." She was such a clever jokester who could always find her humor.

Now that's in me.

One cold day at recess duty, after many years of teaching together, I commented to Sarah that I thought we'd taught our students to be more compassionate than the behavior I was seeing. I pointed out that it appeared that a group of our kids were kicking a ball *at* one of our students, and then running away. Sarah said, "Christine, he's the goalie."

…turns out things aren't always as they appear. Who knew? Sarah did and now that's in me.

When Sarah and I were sharing strategies to help us work with a difficult student or parent, she said she tried to think about what could have happened to them last weekend, or even in their lives, that could have made them act this way.

Sarah was compassionate. Now that's in me.

A troupe of Arrowhead teachers attended St. Mary's for our Masters degree in the 1990s. At one point Kim Ratliff, Linda Jones, Tina Webster, Sarah and I were all attending there and Lynn Hanrahan was teaching there. In Dr. McAnnich's class we learned about constantly challenging the norm, forever shifting our paradigm to pursue best practice teaching. Sarah and I had many intense conversations examining, "Why do we do what we do in the classroom?"

We became smarter together. Now that's in me.

Sarah and I lived through my many family deaths and hers. We handled many career challenges such as the closing of our home at Arrowhead. Sarah was brave. Now that's in me.

Right after Sarah died, I had a dream in which I was in a busy room and heard Sarah's unmistakable voice. When I found her I said, "Sarah, what are you doing here? You are dead."

Sarah responded, "Christine, I told you. I'll always be in you." I asked her if everyone could hear her. She laughed and said, "Of coarse not. I'm dead." We spent the rest of the night talking and laughing. I know she'll always be in me and in all of you whose lives she touched in such a powerful way. She'll be in us and all the people whose lives we touch as well.

> You in me
> Me in you
> One heart.

I want to share a poem from *Amber Was Brave, Essie Was Smart* by Vera Williams. Sarah gave me this book when she moved.

> Amber could write her name in script
> Essie taught her
> But Essie could read hard library books
> Amber could tie her own shoes
> if Essie double tied them for her
> Essie could thread a needle
> cook toasted cheese sandwiches
> make cocoa
> put the lipstick on just right
> when they played dress-up
> Amber was brave
> She could get the grocery man
> to trust them for a container of milk
> though their mother
> couldn't pay him till payday
> Amber wasn't afraid of the rat

Sarah Merdian

in the wall under the sink
or of climbing up in high places
Essie kept their house key in her little purse
but the front door to their building wouldn't even open
unless they both pushed on it hard
Essie was tall and Amber was small
Essie was smart and Amber was brave
Essie and Amber
Amber and Essie

Sarah's inscription in this book read:

You be brave;
I'll be smart,
And then we'll switch.

Sarah I'm trying to be brave right now. I know you are too.

You in me;
Me in you;
One heart.

Karen Papania

How hard it is for me to put my thoughts about Sarah into words on a page. My mind is scattered, my time is often interrupted by other things. And yet, my relationship with Sarah helped to shape the person I am today.

Sarah and I met during our UD Rome semester: Fall of 1979. Her personality intimidated me and yet drew me in. We became friends and stayed close until her death. Yes, our paths were very different. I was raising children and moving all over as part of Mark's medical training. There were years when it felt like Sarah and I were on different planets. Sarah visited every home we ever lived in? Including Quetzaltenango, Guatemala. My kids would get an "Aunt Sarah" fix when she visited: stories, games, conversation with an adult who cherished them and was genuinely interested in all they were into. When I left my family to visit Sarah I got adult conversation (and beverages), the chance to explore little restaurants and bookstores, the opportunity to reconnect with who I was before kids. What a great deal! And as my children graduated and went to the University of Dallas, they became even closer with Sarah, inviting her to their parties, enjoying the luxury of home-cooked meals at Sarah's or fun nights out to downtown restaurants far from Irving. She provided a "home away from home" for my oldest 3 while they were in Dallas and this solidified their relationships with her in a new way.

I can only hope that my family and I brought to Sarah as much joy and laughter as she brought to us. Believe me when I say that each and every one of my kids thought they were "her favorite". Isn't that the sign of a great friend or relative? Of course, Sarah had "favorites" all over the country. I am sure we all thought the same thing!

Sarah and I grew increasingly close after her diagnosis and as her disease progressed.

We talked less about stuff and more about life and even death. I became pregnant with our 7th child at age 47. Not easy. I was worried about my baby, thrown by the idea of immersing myself in raising another baby at my age, anxious about what other people would think and say. Sarah was the perfect person to talk to about all of this. She had been dealing with other peoples' comments and opinions most of her life. Her support and words of wisdom helped me through the very difficult first trimester. She continued to be a great source of comfort throughout my pregnancy and delivery of Sophia Grace. Of course, she was the perfect choice to be my daughter's godmother. When we asked Sarah over the phone, she cried and asked, "Wouldn't we want someone who might be around longer?"

Mark and I assured Sarah that we had prayed about it and really felt convicted about the choice. 2 month old Sophia and I flew to Dallas to meet her godmother. Sarah made the trip to our house for an Easter day baptism in April of 2008. It was a wonderful holiday, filled with friends and family gathered to celebrate the Risen Christ and the baptism of our precious little Sophia. Sarah left from our house to head back to MD Anderson. The news was not good. Things got worse quickly from there.

Sophia and I made another trip to see Sarah for her birthday in the hospital. And though it was not easy having a baby visiting in the hospital, I consider myself blessed to have been a part of that time.

I miss Sarah all the time. I think of her courage and wit, her child-like wonder with the world, her joy in the simple (and extravagant!), her sense of style and of course her ability to connect, connect and connect. She was the master of bringing us all together. Didn't the celebration of her life reflect that perfectly?

Laura Daly

When you go to a small university, it doesn't take long to learn the names of the people who everyone knows. The fabled Sarah Merdian and I crossed paths a few months after she graduated from the University of Dallas. I was a senior there at the time, finishing up my degree in elementary education and Sarah had come back for one more year's work to get her teaching certification. Those shared education classes served as the setting for the foundation of our friendship.

During that year, we spent hours talking and working together on assignments the kind of time that really lets you get to know a person. What they believe. Where they've come from. How their brain works. What their passions are. Time like that is hard to find once you leave college. It was in that precious, protected environment where I learned who Sarah was at her core—a generous, kind, brilliant and level-headed soul who would dedicate her life to making sure that every child she taught would leave her classroom with their dreams imagined, possessing the confidence to accomplish them.

Now, it was in that same year that Sarah and I began to work together at Club Schmitz as waitresses. *That* time formed an altogether different part of our friendship. At Club Schmitz (our second career for the first several years we taught), between schlepping burgers and pouring beer, we'd get a chance two nights a week to debrief from our teaching jobs discussing which students were struggling, whose principal was focused on the wrong stuff, how some textbook was way off base all the ups and downs of being teachers.

More importantly, though, we got to laugh for hours on end at all the hilarious happenings at a bar that attracted everyone from the Dallas Cowboys head coaching staff, to a group of guys coming in for beer and chicken wings after illegal bull-dog fights in East Texas....to every walk of life in between.

And so, in a very short period, a private vocabulary of nicknames, clipped phrases, code words and facial expressions was born. "Sarah. Meet me in the phone booth." "There are 132 rooms in the White House—that's just a guess." "There's a river in San Antonio?" The "ticket-in-every-state" vacation. Rena. Princess. Queen Anne.

With as little as a glance or a single-syllable word, a reference was complete and elicited the same reaction a full story did. Some less-than-satisfactory grade we'd get in a class, an accidental pun a student made, a customer's fashion faux pas, the practical joke that went off perfectly were all boiled down into this abbreviated language that represented hours of events and storytelling, and was a reminder of how we appreciated the world in the same way.

My friendship with Sarah was to become the safest place I've ever been. Though as time passed and we grew into adults with vastly different careers and lives, our paths had been forged together during those first few years of study and service. I always knew that—like her students—if I had a dream, Sarah would encourage me. And I knew, too, that if I was off base on something, she'd let me know with a directness that might intimidate some, but made me feel like someone knew just who I was and intended to help me avoid later regret from a ill-conceived plan or a careless word.

The thing about Sarah, though, is that everyone who knew her could say everything I've said so far. She had so many gifts, but perhaps her most tremendous and special one was connecting deeply with you in a way that created an instant and powerful bond. Somehow she always had time for everyone and whether you needed to laugh, or cry, or blow off steam, she knew how to listen and what to say.

Not a day goes by that I don't see or hear something that makes me think of Sarah. Mostly it's funny stuff I'd love to laugh with her about sometimes I just want a good dose of her perspective. Our friendship is an amalgam of comical situations, crazy road trips, difficult emotional journeys, disappointments, tough lessons learned, little and big victories, and lots of laughing. Thanks to her, I am woven into a rich fabric of people who had the privilege and joy of knowing Sarah. What a wonderful gift to leave us all in her absence, we have each other.

Still. I'd give just about anything to pick up the phone one day and hear, "Rena? It's Queen Anne. Do you have a sec?"

John and Deb Combs

I don't know how we can put into words all that Sarah has meant to us. It is simply not possible. She is woven so deeply into our lives that not a day goes by without something triggering a memory: I was baking Santa Snacks, a family favorite, using her recipe. Van Morrison. Our wedding. Lauren's Baptism (Sarah and Dan as godparents). The children's books that fill our bookshelves, now read to our grandson. *Play That Funky Music White Boy* on our return to Rome with Dan and Charles in 2003. Lauren's wedding! Cardinals in winter.

We miss Sarah dearly, yet thank God that she was a part of our life for as long as she was. What a blessing to have known her and for our children to have grown up knowing her. We miss her wit, and are thankful for Sarah's example of finding the humor and joy in most everything. We miss Sarah the teacher, she taught us all about living and dying, with grace, humor and dignity. We miss having Sarah here with us, and when that gets hard, we pray, and thank God for sharing her with us.

Tom Ballou

Sarah was brilliant, witty, talented, caring, and always found the best in others. She was the life of every party and each encounter with her resulted in laughter; usually to the point of tears. She believed all of her students could and should be successful. Her students delighted in her sense of humor and sincerity.

I had the good fortune of being a student teacher in Sarah's classroom. It was one of those moments where fate or Divine Intervention played a role, and my life continues to be impacted in ways I am still discovering.

Sarah and I spoke for the first time in a meaningful way when I was visiting my parents for Christmas break. She said she had 30 students and needed my help. It did not take long to realize she was being generous. Sarah was as skilled as they come, and she had a true sense of her students. Sarah created magic by coupling high expectations with the belief in each child's ability to succeed. She valued them as people, and that made the difference.

Sarah's wit was something special. On one afternoon, the Arrowhead teachers descended upon the teacher's lounge—a name which has always seemed inappropriate as educators do not have time to "lounge"—a Kindergarten teacher entered the room and said, "I've nailed down my place in Hell." After of few minutes of eating and sharing stories, this teacher got up to leave the room.

Sarah's response, "See ya at Adolph's." The room fell apart. She was visiting in Colorado, after a nice dinner, the waitress brought Sarah fresh strawberries dipped in chocolate. She leaned over and said, 'We are stopping for insulin on the way home, right?"

Melanie, her student, wore a Brown University shirt which was "tie dyed" with a variety of colors. Throughout the day she would express her confusion to Melanie concerning the conflicting message of her shirt. Melanie would roll her eyes and groan, "Oh, Miss Merdian." On Valentine's Day, Sarah wore a red dress. As she opened and read the cards each student had given her, she stapled them to her dress. The kids loved it and her.

Sarah's love for teaching was a part of who she was. She would say she couldn't believe she was paid to do a job she loved so. Her fondness for literature and sharing those selections with students occupied many of her weekends. She would take them to author signings, and she could not wait to share new books with the class. When I am teaching, I often find a book she gave me or share a favorite author of hers I know her legacy continues.

One of Sarah's favorite lessons was taught during fifth grade Colonial History. She produced a glass container jammed with pencils. She explained to the students that the principal had informed the teachers of cuts in the budget, and they would have to pay a $0.10 fee per writing utensil. Some students protested, but she managed to get them into the social studies lesson. As the lesson progressed, some of the students would recognize the parallel between The Stamp Act and "Taxation without Representation" and the pencil fee. Acts like The Boston Tea Party began to take on a special significance. Each year her former students would visit and ask if she had taught the lesson, as they could not wait for their peers to have the experience.

Teaching with Sarah was true symbiosis. It was a team effort— one would finish where the other began. The big day had arrived for a field trip which was the culmination of an environmental science unit. Sarah placed a card on my desk that morning with a quote from Chief Seattle with the message "all things are connected." She stated even though I would not know the full impact of my teaching on this day, the impact would continue for decades. On the final day of student teaching she gave me the book entitled, *Among Schoolchildren*, with the inscription, "Since you are a wonderful teacher, you'll get much from this book. Since you are a wonderful person, you'll see even more. I'm proud to be your colleague and friend." I was not able to speak. Sarah chose the right words at the right time. Now her deep insight and honesty will inspire others with the publishing of her Care Pages. Through her candor, we are able to experience real and uncomfortable situations that leave us in laughter, tears, or both. My hope is her writing will provide encouragement and strength to those facing her challenge. In that way, Sarah will continue to do what she loved…teach.

Brent Hoelscher

Sarah Merdian '82 (Constantin). Passed on August 7 in Dallas, Texas. She was a Master Teacher who taught fifth grade for many years. The following tribute was written by Sarah's friend, Brent Hoelscher '80, and is reprinted with his permission:

"Scattershooting about life, death, and Sarah Merdian. The late Jim Valvano once said that if you laugh, you cry, and you think, you've had a full day. For those of you able to attend the Celebration of Sarah today, you, no doubt, will have a full day. I know I speak for all of us unable to be there in person, we will be there with all of you in spirit. It goes without saying that all of us who knew Sarah, no matter to what extent, were richly blessed. For me, our friendship was a 30+ year running battle of sarcastic jabs and caustic retorts. A battle, by the way, which I happily and admiringly lost, every time. For as you well know, to engage Ms. Merdian in a battle of wits is not unlike trading shots with Roger Federer in tennis...you hit what you believe to be a winner right down the line, only to see the return sail past you into the very corner of the court. Game. Set. Match. The neat thing about being around

UDers in general and Sarah in particular is that she always made me smarter, she made me funnier, she made me better.

The last time I saw Sarah was at the Zeskes 25th anniversary party. We had a chance to sit and chat about the preceding 25 years and the topic got around to cancer. She listened with the genuine interest and concern of a true friend, but it seemed to go beyond that. It was almost as if she was taking notes in preparation for an exam. Cancer would become our primary topic in the ensuing years. We exchanged a number of emails, some private, and some public, via that fascinating and inspiring CarePage (which really needs to be turned into a book). Thank you to Mim and Mary H. and anyone else who helped to make that CarePage happen. We spoke of faith and doubt and how to know whether or not you were doing the right thing. We spoke of two possible outcomes, not life and death, but rather life and life after death. There can never have been a person on earth who had so many people fervently praying for her return to health. For those of you, please do not despair. Those prayers DO work... but only if it is God's will, only if they are in accordance with His plan. Sarah was not dealt the greatest of hands here on earth, but through her intelligence and humor and love, she consistently found herself playing at the winner's table. She is where is she is meant to be now.

Sarah, so long......and save us some seats up there will ya? And just for the record, it's Belle-ville, not Belle-vue."

From Sarah's CarePage

Message Board

~ ~

Posted July 30, 2008

by Karen Hayse (Arrowhead)

Living On...Sarah. There are so many little lives you have yet to touch—you will live on in Christine and me as we teach together these next years. It was a great privilege to be next door to you for one, wonderful 5th grade year. You inspired me in many ways.

Posted July 30, 2008

by Kaitlin Hager

Dear Sarah. You will always be my favorite teacher ever, you touched my life and have continued to touch it in so many ways. I am forever grateful for the many blessings you bestowed upon me: the love of reading, (i still remember the day you said it cost money to go to the bathroom, and dylan suggesting writing a letter he was so angry!), love of learning and love of teachers who eventually become friends. The serenity prayer has become my mantra now:

> God grant me the serenity
> to accept the things I cannot change;
> courage to change the things I can;
> and wisdom to know the difference.

Posted July 30, 2008
   by Jen Scarano
   It is Wednesday afternoon and I wish so much I could give you a hug in person and tell you that there isn't a day I don't think about you in some way. Nicholas enjoys story times so much and a big part of it is how your visit to my classroom one day to read to my students helped me up my read-alouds a notch you kept us all captivated with your voice and expression I had always enjoyed reading aloud to kids, but after your visit it was to a new level. Nicholas begs for books to be read (and he is even beginning to read them on his own) and I always tell him about the person who gave him each book, so yes, he is learning all about you! Many, many thanks for your many, many gifts that will go on and on!

—⌣—

Posted July 27, 2008
   by MaryAnne Fisher
   An Incredible Journey. Yes, you must continue to live your life, for it has indeed been an "Incredible Journey" You have lived your life to the fullest and influenced more people in your 48 years than many of us who are 18 years older!! You have inspired me to take risks and face my fears more than any other person I know. You are indeed my hero.

—⌣—

Posted August 2, 2008
   by Denise Johnson (Arrowhead Mother)
   Sarah, here are a couple of examples of how much you have been in our thoughts and prayers. When Heidi was studying cancer cell biology, she commented that studying was just studying, but knowing you made it (the class) real and urgent to her. She wished that she could just hurry up and be your doctor or a doctor for someone like you.

As Heidi received her white coat at the KU Med Center ceremony for 1st year students Friday afternoon, I was thanking God that she had a grade school teacher who taught her not only to read and love studying but also helped her to believe in herself and care for others. You have planted, watered, and nurtured, so many seeds. Know that not only do those seeds continue to grow, but they are following in your example of planting, watering, and nurturing.

Posted August 3, 2008
by Amanda Fite (Tulsa OK)
You have truly inspired me and humbled me with your words and your journey. Thank you for walking us down a road we'll all travel, and showing us how to do it right. You are a sparkle in the eye of Time. And you truly shine.

Posted August 5, 2008
by Beverly Seat (Shawnee Mission)
Bette, Christine, Lynn, Sheila, Tina & I have purchased a star in your constellation. We have named it "Sarah's Meridian" :-) The highest point of power... not the wrong spelling of your name! We will be raising our glasses to you every chance we get! Love always and forever.

Posted August 6, 2008
by Jill Martin
The face of God and all his love is reflected in you. You are the kingdom of heaven on earth.

Posted August 6, 2008
by Scott Lunsford

Hi Tia!!! Wow!! I totally agree with Matt Combs especially the last few lines. I wish I had the eloquence to write my own lines and not steal from other care page writers, but I just can't find the words. I do hope I have expressed at some point how much our family adores you! You truly are the best and I'm not ready to say good bye. How will I ever get my kids through school without your help on 3rd grade Native American projects, advice about cranky 2nd teachers and uncaring principals, not to mention all the trials and tribulations that are yet to come!!!!!!!!! I told you once that I hope they graduate from high school—I'm really going to need your guidance to make that happen!! I know you are laughing at me right now but it is true!!

Posted August 6, 2008
by Karen Sullivan (Arrowhead)

As I think of you today, I remember the wonderful group of friends who painted tiles and worked together on the mirror for you. If it was possible to look in that mirror right now and see the reflection of all of us and how you have touched our lives, you would see the beauty that is you. Whatever God intended for you on this earth has certainly been surpassed. I know that you will be blessed abundantly for all you have given so unselfishly. You are loved.

Posted August 6, 2008
by Matt Combs (Kansas City)

Hi Angel, What is the definition of having succeeded during our tour of duty on this planet? The definition of success is this; it is that soul who can say that they loved with their whole heart and their whole mind and all their strength and with all their soul.

You, my dear friend, are the one who taught me how to do this. You are the one who seemed most void of judgment. You are the one who seemed to know how to leave arrogance at the curb and take someone right where they were at, at that moment, and build from there. That's exactly what God does. That's exactly how God loves. It doesn't get any better than that Sarah. We can't do anything more powerful while we're here. One of my favorite quotes is this, *"There is nothing more powerful than gentleness and nothing more gentle than true power"*. You are a living example of that quotation in action. You are powerful. You are gentle. Your life is a glorious achievement!

"Soon and very soon", (one of my favorite praise songs) Jesus is going to welcome you into Heaven. He will be standing there with His arms outstretched, His trademark gentle smile on His face, and He will greet you and say, "Well-done my good and faithful servant". While this planet is still blessed with your presence, be joyful, be peaceful, and know that you have accomplished your task with glory! We love you today, tomorrow and forever. We will miss you intensely! But ultimately, after the shock of your absence has lessened, we will revel in the joy and the laughter and the wisdom and the honesty with which you blessed each of our lives. I love you Sarah Merdian.

Thank you for being you.

Posted August 7, 2008
by Libby Fischer-Osborne
Dear Sarah,

We will miss you soooo much. You have been a bright light to so many around you. You touched so many here on earth, you taught us all a great deal about how to live this thing called life.

To Sarah's Family and wonderful close friends, you are blessed to have had Sarah so close to you in your lives. My prayers go to you, I know you are feeling intense sadness yet I'm sure you too are happy that Sarah is out of pain. She will be with all of us and especially you for all of eternity. God Bless each of you. May God bathe you in his Grace. To God and all his Heavenly Angels, Hold Sarah close to you, she is special to all of us. Thank you Sarah for all you are.

Posted August 7, 2009
by Reese Lunsford (niece)

I just wanted to extend my love and warm wishes as we celebrate both a hard day and a day full of memories. I know that we all love Sarah (Tia!!) very much and wish that she was still here with us. I know that she is in a better place, without suffering, filled with family and friends that have gone before us and the ability to touch us each and every day in a way that was not possible to her before. Use today as a day to celebrate a wonderful woman and remember all the laughs that we shared.

Tia, I love you very much. Thank you for all the things that you have done for me and that you will continue to do. Give Mommom and Grandpa a kiss for me and extend my love to them as well.

Posted August 7, 2008—11:34pm
by Kathy Schulte

The world really is a better place because you've been in it. You have changed so many lives that would have never been changed for the better otherwise. Although it had been a long time since we had seen one another, I hold so many great memories in my heart of you. There were so many good laughs and conversations. I only wish so much that there could be more. I am glad though for you that you are finally free of your pain here. God bless you Sarah and to your family.

Posted August 7, 2008

by Rob Montgomery (Pascagoula, MS)

Sarah, I never knew you personally, but you have inspired me to live my life fully, through your witty writing and constant giving to others.

—⁓—

Posted August 7, 2008

by Sibyl Koss (Uplift Peak)

Although I did not know you for long I felt like we were long time friends. What you accomplished with the children and those who knew you was more than thousands of people put together. Your powerful humor and your work will always be admired and used as an example for future teachers, parents and students.

—⁓—

Posted August 7, 2008

by Chris McGehee (UD Alum)

To all of you who shared even a brief moment in time with this extraordinary lady, I recall the words of Dan Utrecht, who shared the following words with many of us years ago in a similar time of shared pain and grief: *"A great light has been taken from our midst, not that we may be cast into darkness; rather, each of us is now called to shine that much brighter".* May we bring a smile to Sarah as we share that light with all we encounter. While so many of you were dear to Sarah, I want to especially mention Dan and Charles. No greater example of true friendship, in thick or thin, could ever be provided us. Thank you my friends. I close amidst tears of joy and thanksgiving. Joy in the certainty of Sarah's presence in the arms of Christ, and thanksgiving that she rests beyond the dominion of bodily pain. Our love flies with you to heaven.

—⁓—

Posted August 7, 2008
by Dawn Osborne

It is with an equally heavy heart that we hear this news. May she live an eternity in peace, tranquility, but with the joyful laughter she was good at creating in every situation. I am so thankful to have been touched by her and to have had the opportunity to see such a talented and dedicated teacher work her own special kind of miracles everyday. She blessed so many. Now, may she reap those same blessings.

—~—

Posted August 7, 2008
by Milton Olsen, MD (Tulsa, OK)

I have learned more about life and living for each moment from this brave warrior angel. May God Most High bless and comfort Sarah's family, close friends, and all who were touched in some way by her marvelous, beautiful life.

—~—

Posted August 7, 2008
by Kay Heley (former student)

Dear Ms. Merdian, I want to thank you for being my teacher way back in fifth grade. I am going to be a sophomore now, but I still can remember some of the fun things we did in the fifth grade. The Stamp Act, the 20th Century project (my group was the 40's with Layne Rieder and Bryan Wood), and We the People. I was watching the Simpsons' yesterday and there was an episode where Lisa stole every teacher's edition in the school, so the teachers didn't have any answers. The teachers, of course, didn't know what to do. But you never seemed to need those books, because you taught us things that aren't in the teacher's edition. You taught us how it felt to be taxed unfairly. You showed us pictures from your trip to Egypt. You made us learn our spelling words using a tic-tac-toe board! I hope you live peacefully, because you deserve it. For all the kids you ever taught and inspired, I thank you.

—⟡—

Posted August 7, 2008

by Kay Heley (Arrowhead Mother)

Logan and I were in Florida this past week and as I looked out at the infinite expanse of water with the constant rhythmic lapping of the waves and the gorgeous sunset behind, I felt peace for you. There is so much we cannot understand about our lives. There is so much we will never know about the impact our lives have had. This particular life of yours has been a life well-lived and one with great impact on many, many people. Thank you for your example and your time with our family. Thoughts of peace, love, warmth, and light to surround you in comfort.

—⟡—

Posted August 8, 2009

by Juan J Hernandez (former student)

I wrote this message prior to knowing of her passing... Rest in Peace Ms. Merdian.

Hi Ms. Merdian!

This is Juan Hernandez! One of your former students from St. Cecilia School! I just wanted to say hi and let you know that you are still my favorite teacher! I am currently a teacher (inspired by you) in San Antonio! I taught in Oak Cliff for 7 years, and I am now in San Antonio teaching 2nd grade. I am currently attending TSU to attain my PhD in School Improvement. I want to go back to Oak Cliff when I'm done and create a school with my brother, Macario. You've inspired me for many years and continue to do so! I remember your humor and down-to-earth-ness. If you're still in Dallas, I hope I'm reaching you. Take care and you'll always be in my prayers and thoughts. Con mucho amor.

—⟡—

Posted August 8, 2008
   by MaryAnne Fisher

As another member of Sarah's "Arrowhead Family", I, too, want to send my deepest sympathy to her mother, sister, and other family members and friends. Sarah was an incredible person and the greatest teacher I've ever known...she could teach anyone and never gave up on a student! I remember when she joined the staff at Arrowhead and she was so impressed that the school district provided her with notepads, a mug, and other articles with her initials on them...SM. Indeed, Sarah Merdian was a very important part of the Shawnee Mission school district, and when she left it, she was greatly missed, as she will be missed here on earth by all of us who loved her so!

Posted August 8, 2008
   by Karen Sullivan (Arrowhead Family/Shawnee Mission)

To Sarah's mother, sister and incredible friends and caregivers in Texas: I am so very sorry for your loss but want to thank you from afar for the love, caring, support and laughs you shared with Sarah throughout her "INF" journey. This journey is not finished and now we can extend it with our memories of Sarah and just how much she touched our lives.

Posted August 8, 2008
   by Carole and Rick Carter (Arrowhead/Shawnee Mission)

Our deepest condolences to Sarah's mother, Jane, sister, Monica, and to Mary, Laura, Charles and all her friends who surrounded her with such devoted love and caring. The world is a brighter place for Sarah having been here and we are so thankful that we were able to know her and be touched by her special love and caring.

Posted August 9, 2008

by Chester Perry (cancer survivor MD Anderson)

What a wonderful person Sarah was and the light she showed to others thru her ordeal. My wife and i pray for her and her family through this tough time.

Posted August 10, 2008

by Suzy Edmonson (Baylor Pain Management Team)

Bless you, Sarah Godspeed! I am praying that so many loving family members and friends be surrounded and infused with God's love, peace, and strength. I know Sarah is, as well, in abundance!

Posted August 10, 2008

by Loretta Barta (Cousin)

Sarah indeed touched many lives throughout her time here on earth. She was such a kind, loving person with such a terrific sense of humor. She always amazed me how she as well as her sister Monica were so quick witted. Sarah continued to amaze with her hidden strength to fight this cancer as she did. She gave it her all. We will all miss her smile and always her sense of encouragement. We all can learn from her experience to never give up. Love you Sarah always and may you be blessed as we have been blessed by having you in our family.

Posted August 11, 2008

by Tom Hansell (UD alum Mary's husband)

Sarah, you are an exquisite and beautiful flower. We had the privilege to witness your life on earth. You are a rare comedy of profound depth, subtle nuance, and outrageously human hilarity.

We were taught your lessons, we felt your love, we witnessed your beauty, and we were blessed by God's grace within you. We are, each one of us, God bless us all, far better for having known you Sarah, do not worry you are not finished. We are your students, your friends, and your family. We promise, you live on within us.

⌣

Posted August 11, 2008

by MaryDent Grieve ovarian cancer survivor 3 years. Palm Bay, Fl and Newport, WA

Sarah will be missed. I only knew Sarah through her CarePages website and only for a short time, and I will miss her.

⌣

Posted August 12, 2008

by Susan Klaber (a grateful Mom)

Thank you to everyone who cared for and loved Ms. Merdian, as she was known around our house... She was my son and daughter's fifth grade teacher in Kansas.

Ms. Merdian was the first and only teacher to allow my son (who had ADHD) do less repetitions of homework problems so that we would not be up until 10 or 11pm fighting over completing his homework. She was an absolute angel in my eyes! I even sent her name and info in to suggest she be selected as a TEACHER OF THE YEAR candidate.

She was an amazing individual with incredible strength and character. She was able to share a very difficult and trying time in her life with honesty and humor. I am so thankful that she allowed me (us) to share with her in her journey the last year and a half.

To those left behind (for now) please know how much she was admired, respected, and appreciated for who she was as a person, friend, and teacher. I share in your sense of loss, yet feel totally blessed to have been able to share in a part of her incredible life! May God comfort you in this time of immeasurable loss.

— ~

Posted August 16, 2008—11:53pm
    by Kim Ratliff (Arrowhead)

To Miss Jane, Monica, and all of Sarah's family and family of friends, thank you for sharing her with us. I am so sorry for your loss, our loss, and know that your pain is shared. She did not just teach children, she taught me how to be a better friend, a better teacher, and a better person. There will never be another Sarah.

— ~

www.SarahMerdian.com